the

Black Powder
PLAINSMAN

A Beginner's Guide to Muzzle-Loading and
Reenactment on the Great Plains

the

Black Powder
PLAINSMAN

A Beginner's Guide to Muzzle-Loading and
Reenactment on the Great Plains

RANDY SMITH

Skyhorse Publishing

Skyhorse Publishing books may be purchased in bulk at special discounts for sales promotion, corporate gifts, fund-raising, or educational purposes. Special editions can also be created to specifications. For details, contact the Special Sales Department, Skyhorse Publishing, 307 West 36th Street, 11th Floor, New York, NY 10018 or info@skyhorsepublishing.com. Skyhorse® and Skyhorse Publishing® are registered trademarks of Skyhorse Publishing, Inc.®, a Delaware corporation.

Visit our website at www.skyhorsepublishing.com.

10 9 8 7 6 5 4 3 2 1
Library of Congress Cataloging-in-Publication Data is available on file.

ISBN: 978-1-61608-286-4

Printed in China

Contents

Acknowledgments

SO MUCH HAS HAPPENED SINCE THIS BOOK WAS FIRST PUBLISHED. Most of the names you will read here are no longer with us. These people sent me on a course of writing and black powder hunting that has taken me around the world. Several were and are very good friends. They always will be.

Special thanks must go to Bill Gwaltney of the National Park Service for the early encouragement and connections for my original research. Juanita Leisch provided a core of knowledge for my research on women of the 19th century. William Brown provided invaluable research on men's clothing. Turner Kirkland of Dixie Gunworks and Val Forgett of Navy arms unselfishly worked with me on black powder arms history. My old friend, Dr. Gary White of Roosevelt, Utah, helped me develop a philosophy of muzzleloader ethics and provided me with international hunting opportunities that would not have otherwise been possible. Butch Winters of Dixie Gunworks, Linda Scurlock of Rebel Publishing, Sharon Cunningham of Dixie Gunworks, Wolfgang Droeg of Shiloh Mfg., Johathan Mullius of Uberti, USA, Linda DeProfio of Sturm, Ruger & Company, C. B. Tuschick and later Tom Hall of Traditions Inc., and Laina Hertz of Connecticut Valley Arms provided support and research material.

I will never forget my first rendezvous. I came alone and green without knowing a single person. I was greeted with smiles, friendly conversation, and good-natured advice. I had not experienced such open and friendly spirit. So to Bear, Sidemeat, Slim, Granny, Bill, Dishes, Cat Woman, Buck, and hundreds of others like them, I express my respect and admiration. I hope this book does for others what they did for me.

Randy D. Smith – 2012

1

The Hobby of Muzzle-Loading

IT IS SOMETIMES DIFFICULT TO EXPLAIN THE APPEAL OF BLACK powder and muzzle-loading to a person who has not really felt or expressed an interest in guns. Perhaps the reason is that most people try to keep the subject gun-oriented in nature. The difficulty is that the hobby involves more than that. Yes, muzzle-loading begins normally with a gun. Often, on impulse, a person will walk

Friendly Game—Finding shade from the sun, reenactors enjoy a game of dominos. The man on the right wears a flannel overshirt, typical dress of a southwestern trapper. The leather shoes and more formal dress of his companion suggest the attire of a tradesman.

into a store with a few extra bucks in his pocket and satisfy a curiosity that has been gnawing at his insides by purchasing a black powder weapon off the rack or in kit form. Many will put the kit together, take the new gun out, and shoot it a few times before stuffing it in a closet or hanging it on the wall and forgetting about it.

People often pay premium prices at auctions for black powder replicas with no greater intention than simply to hang them in the den or over the fireplace. That seems fine for some, but for someone like me, it is a waste. It is true that black powder weapons are pieces of beauty. That is especially true in our age of ultra-modern, stamped-out military rifles, awkward parabellum pistols, and other similar unemotional machines.

Black powder replicas and originals, by contrast, recall another age with different values and priorities. Heavy metal construction, beautiful woodwork, and smooth-flowing classic lines that seem to invite inspection are hallmarks of most black powder weapons. They speak of art, craftsmanship, and pride.

Open Country Shooting—The plains represent a unique challenge for muzzle-loading. Extreme distances create shooting challenges.

Black powder weapons just seem to naturally align themselves with old barns, primitive art, and doing things the way that Grandpa did. They seem to tell modern man to slow down, relax, and enjoy life a little bit. Few people are around black powder weapons for long without succumbing to the urge to touch them. They feel good. Many seem made for the hand. Their lines draw a person to them for closer inspection. They cry out to be fired and used. Hanging them on the wall seems such a terrible waste for something that was meant to do so much more.

These old-time weapons speak of past ages. The mind tends to naturally say to itself, "So this is what they used," or, "This is how it felt." The idea of facing hostile attack or having to put food on the table with these slow-loading, somewhat unreliable, and at times fickle weapons suggests a courage and determination of the men who use them that seems lacking in our modern society. These men and women came from a world where answers and challenges were more elemental than those of today. Gone are microwave ovens, data processing, cholesterol counts, toxic wastes, and nine-to-five pressure cooker job environments. The world that is recalled was no less dangerous or frustrating. In fact, the life-and-death struggle was much greater than it is now. But a world of "use it up and throw it away" seems the poorer by contrast. Possessions of this earlier time were to be taken care of and made to last, often through more than one generation. There is an appeal here for many of us. The old world of "make do and make it good" stands in sharp contrast to today's world of rush and crowds and indifference. This is only part of the appeal of muzzle-loading.

There are muzzle-loading weapons that are designed strictly for taking advantage of modern hunting seasons. There are a few that are just as shoddily built for quick profit as are other products of our modern society. As a result of the excellent competition in today's muzzle-loading arms industry, the shoddy products just don't last long. No matter how modern a manufacturer may make a muzzleloader in appearance and fell, it can't get away from that one-at-a-time, take-your-time, and do-it-right element that prevails in the world of muzzle-loading weapons.

More Than Just Guns

We do move beyond the gun-oriented element of the argument that I mentioned earlier. Even though the gun may be where a hobbyist begins, it doesn't take long to move on to other worlds. Art, history, science, nature, and philosophy become a part of the hobby when a person becomes more involved. The small number of questions that arose upon first examination keeps growing. How did they do this? How did they do that? What did they do when they were faced with this situation or that problem? Questions of clothing, health, food preparation, and mere survival keep growing in the mind. Answers can sometimes be found through reading or experience. At other times, good old common sense must be employed.

Buffalo Bill—William F. Cody is the most famous of the plainsmen. Buffalo hunter, pony express rider, scout, guide, and showman, he lived his life and made his fortune from his experiences on the plains. His ranch can be visited near North Platte, Nebraska. (*Courtesy Santa Fe Trail Center*)

It is a natural outgrowth for an active muzzleloader to become a student of history. This is not the "names and dates" kind of history that often bores students into unconsciousness in our schools. It is rather a hands-on living history that examines the little things that our forefathers experienced. I have found myself suddenly interested in odd subjects like quilts, shoes, harnesses, window design, cooking, sewing, wood carving, furniture, crockery, medicine, and thousands of other things that I once took for granted. I have been drawn into a world of old that helps me appreciate a world of new. People who were once just history or English class reading assignments are now real with real problems, strengths, and weaknesses.

The Rebirth of Black Powder

Muzzle-loading never did entirely die out during the late 19th and early 20th centuries. There have always been a small number of shooters and historians interested in the weapons and ideas that I have expressed. But for many years the sport was limited to those people who had the money to buy expensive antiques or custom-made replicas, or were fortunate

Buffalo Bill Reenactor—Kirk Shapland, a reenactor known for his portrayal of William F. Cody, presents at Buckskin Joe in Colorado.

enough to have access to an old muzzleloader that had been forgotten in some family closet or shed. When I was a youth, my grandfather had an old double-barrel shotgun in his bedroom closet that was just such a treasure. The family didn't trust the gun. As much as I wanted to shoot it, the beautiful old weapon was declared off-limits. The shotgun was considered an attractive nuisance that might kill or cripple. One of my grown cousins finally purchased the romantic old heirloom with the strict promise that it would be a wall hanger. It was probably just as well. In my ignorance I might have ruined that old guardian of untold numbers of express boxes, as well as myself.

Availability changed muzzle-loading from an obscure hobby to a national sport. Two men are given credit for having the foresight and the courage to try to market something that didn't appear at the time to have much potential. In the mid-1950s, Turner Kirkland of Union City, Tennessee, began marketing a simple little muzzleloader called the New Dixie Squirrel Rifle. His early enterprise has grown to become the largest black powder service in the world. At the present time, Dixie Gun Works sends out over 65,000 catalogs each year to the growing ranks of black powder devotees.

At about the same time, a young many named Val Forgett began marketing replicas of Civil War vintage cap and ball revolvers under the name of Navy Arms Company. Mr. Forgett wrote me stating that under the banner of Classic Arms, Ltd. in the late 1970s and early 1980s, the company was producing 10,000 pistols and kits a month. He estimated that it was probably the largest production of guns in America at that time. Both Val and Turner are gone now but Dixie Gun Works and Navy Arms are doing quite nicely today, having sold more muzzleloaders than Colt, Remington, or Derringer ever did.

Though his early product was not a muzzleloader, partial credit should also go to Bill Ruger of Sturm, Ruger & Co. During the Western television craze of the 1950s, Ruger introduced a single-action revolver to provide an alternative to the growing scarcity of the Colt single-action Peacemaker. It is very possible that Ruger's success helped inspire Kirkland and Forgett to make their attempts at marketing more primitive types of weapons.

Categories of Muzzle-Loading

It appears that the hobby of muzzle-loading can be divided into three distinct categories. Each of these three can provide an interesting hobby within its own limitations and it is this variability that gives muzzle-loading such a strong future.

On the first level are the kit builder and collector. Even in the largest cities, where shooting is limited, this hobbyist can satisfy his interest in antique weapons. Where originals are often priced in the thousands of dollars, the average hobbyist can own replica arms at a fraction of the cost. If that person enjoys working

Hunting with a Muzzleloader—Muzzleloader hunting is exciting and challenging, resulting in enormous growth over the past thirty years.

with his hands, kits can be purchased for even less money. After a few enjoyable evenings, the kit builder can produce a beautiful replica or reproduction of a classic historical firearm. From what I have witnessed, this is one hobby where the value of the item can be increased if the kit builder takes his time and does it right. Fancy presentation boxes for these replicas are also available for purchase or in kit form. A very impressive gift or possession can be created if a hobbyist is willing to work with his piece and give it a bit of attention. It can be a very enjoyable and relaxing interest.

The second aspect of the hobby is that of hunting and shooting. Today a serviceable replica muzzleloader that is capable of superior accuracy and taking big game can be purchased for about the same price as an average-quality .22 caliber rifle. This reasonable price structure has opened up black powder shooting to the common man. Muzzleloaders are legal and special hunting seasons exist in all states.

Most of today's muzzle-loading arms producers are aiming their products at this hunting trade. Estimates place the number near twenty-five million. With even a conservative estimate of one in ten of these hunters using muzzleloaders, one can see excellent marketing possibilities. As urban civilization spreads and practical shooting ranges continue to be limited through legislation, an increase in muzzle-

The Kit Advantage—Muzzleloader kits are inexpensive and functional. Kits can be customized to meet reenactment needs or as a hobby. Fit and finish are limited only to skill and patience. (*Courtesy Traditions Inc.*)

loading interest could take place. It seems odd that primitive weapons can benefit from such modern conditions, but it does make for a bright future for the muzzle-loading hunter.

Primarily among other inherent qualities, the muzzle-loading hunter finds himself becoming more of a naturalist and student of the habits of his quarry. Like the archery hunter or trout angler, the muzzleloader hunter becomes involved in a thinking game where he has to place himself in a much more advantageous situation to make up for the one-shot limit he has placed upon himself. At ranges of less than 100 yards, I do not believe there is a muzzleloader power handicap. The efficiency of the .50 or .54 caliber muzzleloader is awesome at short range. A muzzleloader is not capable of matching the extended range of a modern high-powered rifle. To overcome this range limitation, the hunter is required to stalk his game. He must place his shot accurately because he has only one. His clean kill zone is significantly reduced when compared to even the lower-powered modern centerfire cartridges. I find myself passing up shots that I would have attempted with modern weapons. If taking game is the sole goal,

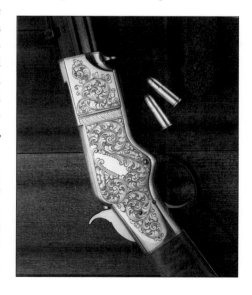

Works of Art—Many are attracted to historical arms because of the beauty and craftsmanship involved in production. This Henry replica is a beautiful example of modern reproduction. (*Courtesy Uberti USA*)

the muzzleloader is a poor choice. If evening the odds and pitting your skills against your quarry is important, a historical replica muzzleloader may be a perfect choice.

Finally, there is the living history or reenactment element of muzzle-loading. Although this is an important avenue and is normally associated with shooting, it is also necessary to note that one can be involved in living history and never go near a weapon. The rifle or pistol might draw a person into reenactment but often the gun is literally left behind if reenactment interests grow. This part of the hobby can get expensive if allowed to go to extremes. However, as will be seen in a later chapter, the costs can be kept quite reasonable if the outfit and activities are kept simple. And it is great fun! There is a comradery involved in this activity that exists in few others. Kindred spirits gathering together for some fellowship and fun is its main attraction. Whereas hunting and craft-making can be very personal, it just isn't much fun coming up with an historical outfit or skill and not having someone to share it with. It is a natural outgrowth of owning a historical weapon, which is why the two activities seem so closely linked together.

Categories of Living History

At the present time there are four areas of living history that are being enjoyed with replica firearms in the United States. One is the early America and American Revolution time period. The Eastern longhunter and colonial soldier are examples of this period.

A second area consists of Civil War reenactments. This is especially popular in the areas where the Civil War was fought.

A third element is the mountain man and rendezvous interest, which empha-sizes the fur traders and trappers of the Far West. This group enjoyed significant growth for several years, probably due to the popularity of the Hawken or Plains Rifle in modern-day black powder hunting.

The fourth element is the recent rebirth of the cowboy as a popular image in America. This resurgence of interest has led to the growth of Old West gunslinger and shooting activities. The cowboy legend has always been enormously popular in this country, but only lately has there been a determined effort to accurately portray the cowboy as he really was. For years the cowboy was lost in a conglomeration of dress styles and time periods.

The 1873 Colt and the 1892 Winchester rifle have been commonly depicted as representative weapons for the time period from 1836 to 1936. Only in the last few years has there been a determined effort among aficionados to get things right in the portrayal of the Western lifestyle. Part of the fun of going to a Western movie was to see how accurate the costumes really were. Many of you reading this know what I mean: Indians shooting Winchesters and riding modern saddles with a blan-ket thrown over them for effect; women who always look like they just stepped out of the shower and are covered with makeup, wearing designer hairstyles on the old Oregon Trail; and perhaps the worst offenders—Roy Rogers, Gene Autry and Hopalong Cassidy—living a 1940s lifestyle in an 1870s setting are all examples of what I am talking about. Many of us grew up with Roy, Gene, and Hoppy and will always have a soft spot in our hearts for all three, but accurate they weren't. In many ways, they do an injustice to our brave ancestors who settled and civilized the American West.

The Common Meeting Ground

When a person studies American history and examines the locations and time periods involved, there is one location and period where the Civil War soldier, the mountain man, and the early cowboy come together. It was a time when the Indian was more or less competitive and frequently clashed with the settlers on the

Rendezvous Meeting—These rendezvous participants are comparing tools, equipment, and outfits at the Rocky Mountain College rendezvous.

plains. It was a time of trial and tribulation, a time when the king of weaponry was the muzzle-loading rifle and handgun. It took place from roughly 1820 to 1873 and was located on the great open western plains of the United States. During this period the country fought the Texas Rebellion and a great war with Mexico, settled and established the borders of our country, destroyed the great American bison herds, and pushed the American Indian into his last desperate stand. America fought a civil war and built the first transcontinental railroads.

It was the time of Sam Houston, Kit Carson, the Pony Express, Dodge City, and the great cattle drives on the Chisholm Trail. It began with the opening of the Santa Fe trade, ran through the Civil War, and ended with the Battle of the Little Big Horn in 1876. It was the time of the Santa Fe Trail and the day of the black powder plainsman. It is to this time and location that a great deal of this book will be devote.

2

The Days of the Santa Fe Trail

THE WORLD THAT EXISTED ON THE PLAINS OF THE OLD WEST IN the year 1830 was much different that that of today. James Monroe was the fifth President of the United States. There were only twenty-two states, mostly huddled east of the Mississippi River. Before the end of the year, Missouri would join the Union as a slave state. Daniel Boone was enjoying the eighty-fifth and final year of his life on a family homestead in Missouri. Thirteen-year-old Robert Edward Lee was spending his time in school with friends while his widowed mother struggled to survive financially. A recent development in firearms technology was the five-year-old concept of the percussion cap, which seemed to be gaining some acceptance over the flintlock. The Great Plains were commonly called "The Great American Desert."

The Big Trail—Throughout the history of the Plains, ox trains such as this from the 1929 motion picture *The Big Trail* were common. Oxen were cheap and dependable, especially when grass was the most common feed for the animals. (*Courtesy Santa Fe Trail Center*)

The **Santa Fe Trail** was mainly a trade route and was the first major trail across the Plains. It followed the Arkansas River as much as possible in dry seasons.

The **Smokey Hill Trail** worked its way into the gold fields of Colorado and followed the Smokey Hill River.

The **Mormon** and **Oregon Trails** followed the Plate River and were the major imigration trails of the late 1840's and 1850's.

After the Civil War, the **Chisholm Trail** was followed by money-hungry Texans as they drove their cattle north to the westward advancing railroad.

(Courtesy Kansas Heritage Center)

America's neighbor to the west, Spain, held to a strict Anglo-stay-out policy as the government tried to maintain a precarious hold on its vast empire in the Americas. The Spanish controlled an area that stretched throughout Central and South America and ventured as far north as present-day Oregon. The first rendezvous of the Rocky Mountain fur trade was still five years away and a bankrupt Missourian by the name of Moses Austin was trying to convince his twenty-six-year old son, Stephen, to take up a land grant that had finally been approved for a colony in Spanish Texas.

There were two million Americans west of the Appalachians and they were ready to move further west onto the plains just as soon as someone could figure out how to make a living on this endless grassland that seemed fit only for about forty million buffalo and a few Indians.

Enter the Americans

In 1821, a failed merchant by the name of William Becknell decided that he had an answer to his problems. Doing his best to escape creditors, he decided to take a string of pack horse loaded with knives, needles, fabrics, and a few pots and pans from his home in Franklin, Missouri, and go out on the prairie to trade with the Cheyenne. The only problem was that he couldn't find any Cheyenne. He followed the Arkansas River as far west as he could into modern day Colorado,

Early Chaps—This plainsman reenactor at Bent's Fort, Colorado, is wearing leggings of leather over cool cotton muslin pants. This is an early form of post-Civil War cowboy chaps.

then swung south into what he thought was hostile Spanish territory. Eventually he ran into some Mexican soldiers who told him that they had kicked the Spanish out. They then asked why he wanted to trade all that good stuff to Indians when there were lots of Mexicans who needed it worse and would pay better. It sounded good to Becknell so he went down to Santa Fe and made nearly a 900 percent profit on his goods.

Old William decided that trading with the Mexicans was pretty good for his bank account. He figured he would make a second trip with a wagon. He also decided that rather than going as far west along the Arkansas as before, he would swing southwest at a point about 150 miles west of the big bend of the Arkansas and make for the Cimarron River, cutting several hundred miles off of the journey.

While in Santa Fe, Becknell ran into a young fellow by the name of Joe Walker who had been cooling his heels in jail for two years for trying the same thing before the Spanish had been kicked out. Walker had gotten out of jail by coming up with a scheme to fight Pawnees who had been raiding the New Mexicans. He had received special trading concessions for his efforts. Becknell went on to become known as the "Father of the Santa Fe Trail" and Walker became what many consider to be the greatest of the mountain men.

In 1823, Becknell made a second trip to Santa Fe and another 900 percent profit. Meanwhile, a fellow by the name of William Ashly organized a trading trip into the high Rockies of the Wind River. He took at least seven young men with him. Among this group were such adventurers as Jedediah Smith, Jim Bridger, Tom Fitzpatrick, Hugh Glass, Bill and Milton Sublette, Ed Rose, and Jim Clyman. They found plenty of Indians and hundreds of mountain streams filled with beaver. At that time, beaver pelts were the closest thing to gold that there was. With the vigorous trade in Santa Fe and the riches of the mountains to the north just waiting for the taking, the race across the plains began. It would begin the fifty-year lifespan of the Santa Fe trade and one of the greatest periods of American history.

The Glorified West—This popular painting of Jedediah Smith provides an entertaining image of the early 1800s. (*Courtesy Bookings College*)

Major Trails of the Plains

In the early years of the 19th century, life on the Santa Fe, especially over an open stretch of waterless plains called the *Jornada de Muerto*, could get pretty dry. The availability of water was always the first concern of any traveler. During the same period that Becknell was active, another band was forced to kill their dogs, cut off the ends of their mules' ears, and suck the blood for moisture just to stay alive. Because of these constantly dry conditions, most of the main trails across the plains tended to follow the rivers. The Santa Fe followed the Arkansas. To the north, the later Mormon and Oregon trails followed the Platte. Between them was the Smoky Hill Trail following, naturally enough, the Smoky Hill River. The Missouri River was the natural course to follow across the plains to the Northwest Pacific region.

The Indian's Clash with White Culture

White settlements clung to these rivers for years for protection and the Indians were forced out onto the grasslands. Even the Indians hadn't fared too well on this open country. They usually stayed out of it until some careless Spanish settlers lost or traded away some horses, giving the Indians a new lease on life. With the coming of the horse, Indian civilization flourished on the Plains. No longer did the tribes have to wait for the semiannual coming of the buffalo. They were mobile for the first time and could follow the herds. They built their whole economy around the horse and the buffalo. Much like the Mongol of ancient Asia, they became raiders and warriors.

Although the Plains Indians never rivaled the great agricultural civilization of Mexico or the Mississippi in grandeur, they certainly did in splendor. For 200 years they ruled the prairie and plains

The Real West—A man caught on the Plains was often the victim of Indian reprisals. This scalped bison hunter was found near Larned, Kansas, on the Santa Fe Trail. (*Courtesy Santa Fe Trail Center.*)

from Mexico to Canada. A great Indian corridor existed, with Anglos gaining a foothold on either end. As long as the whites stayed out, the Indian's lifestyle worked well. But after the Civil War, a second wave of exploration of the American continent by the whites was under way.

From that point on, the Plains Indian found himself under constant harassment that was the beginning of the end of his civilization. He staged a valiant resistance but time, numbers, and a growing technological disadvantage worked against him. Struggle as he might, it was just a matter of time until he was crushed by the advance of a much more modern civilization.

The Mountain Men and the Plains

The two decades from 1820 to 1840 were the era of the mountain man. In his constant search for rich, new beaver trapping grounds, his kind explored most of the Rocky Mountains that stretched across the western third of North America. This incredible feat of exploration was even more heroic when one considers the fact that these men were almost totally isolated from the eastern part of the country and civilization by the expanse of the Plains.

One man or a small group of trappers might survive in the relative protection of the mountains, but to venture out on the open prairie alone was almost certain suicide. Whites crossed this open natural barrier in groups. They needed sizable force to withstand attack. The recommended number was usually a 100. The fact that muzzle-loading weapons of the age were simply too slow to reload made it virtually impossible for a single man to withstand a serious attack from increasing hostile natives.

The Growth and Influence of Texas

While the mountain man was enjoying his shining times, another wave of settlement was taking place in the South. The colony that Moses Austin had founded in the eastern part of Texas was growing and taking on a personality of its own. Austin had passed away before the colony was

Protector of the Plains—Fort Larned reenactor portrays a 10th Cavalry soldier. The 10th was an African American unit that served extensively on the Plains and in the Southwest.

barely on its feet. His son, Stephen, had taken over leadership and was bringing hundreds of families into the lightly settled but potentially rich territory that would become Texas. In return for becoming Mexican citizens and agreeing to adopt the Roman Catholic faith, a man could gain a sizable acreage for settlement.

Though it didn't trust the independent and stubborn *americanos*, the Mexican government tolerated their advance, largely because its own feudal system of settlement and government didn't work well so far from Mexico City. The government saw these ambitious Americans as the most expedient means of settling the dangerous lands that made up the far northern end of its empire.

From the beginning, it was an uneasy alliance at best. The more Anglos there were in texas, the less loyal the population became toward Mexico. It only took fifteen years for relations to break down completely. In spite of their pledges, the Americans did not think of themselves as either Mexican or Roman Catholic. They were simply too independent to accept the paternalistic and alien leadership of a government that existed so far from them in both distance and philosophy.

By 1835, the Texans were in open rebellion. The Mexican dictator, Antonio de Santa Anna, decided to take a large force and punish the Texans for their disobedience. The Texans rallied under the leadership of a hard-drinking, combative Tennessee ex-governor named Sam Houston. While Houston tried to organize his forces, Texas reeled under the surge of Santa Anna's onslaught. The Texans underwent major defeats at Goliad and a small mission near San Antonio called the Alamo. Eventually the distance and supply problems that had hindered the Mexican settlement of Texas from the beginning began to plague Santa Anna. As his supply lines and reinforcements became strung out over this stretch of low, open prairie land, the dictator's advance slowed to a crawl. He was meeting very little resistance from the Texans and possibly felt that he had already fought and defeated the best opposition that the hard-pressed rabble would be able to muster.

In late April 1836, Santa Anna rested his advance guard near a swampy bog called San Jacinto. It was there that Houston and a rag-tag force of 800 frontiersmen delivered a crushing blow to the Mexicans. In a surprise attack that lasted less than thirty minutes, the vengeful Texans completely routed the Mexican force. When it was over, Santa Anna was Houston's prisoner and Texas was on its way toward independent nation status.

For the next ten years, the resource-rich but cash-poor Texans struggled against Indian harassment and Mexican reprisal. For much of their defense the Texans relied on a minuteman type of organization known as the Texas Rangers. To help make up for the Rangers's weakness in numbers, they were issued a fragile little five-shot .34 caliber revolving pistol manufactured in Paterson, New Jersey. Invented by a clever young man named Sam Colt, the revolver was much like Texas itself. It seemed like a good idea but needed time to grow to perfection.

The revolver company failed and the Texas nation almost did as well. In 1845, Texas joined the Union and Sam Colt's idea for a revolving pistol was about to get a second chance.

Mexico was being drawn into the United States as American leadership pushed the boundaries of Texas to the banks of the Rio Grande. As the war raged, many American officers were impressed by the firepower of the Paterson Colts that some Rangers were carrying. A young Texan, Captain Sam Walker, was sent to contact Colt about designing a more powerful and dependable revolver. What resulted from this collaboration was a weapon that would change the face of armed conflict throughout the Plains. A man armed with two of Colt's revolvers could deliver twelve powerful, rapid-fire shots in as many seconds. Although its range was not equal to a rifle, it was devastating in the close range, violent encounters favored by the Indians.

Second Wave of Settlement

The Americans soundly defeated the Mexicans in a short, savage war. Mexico was forced to sell almost all of its empire in what is now the southwester quarter of the United States.

Gold was discovered in California and the government encouraged the settlement of the Oregon territory. Trails of commerce and settlement began snaking their way across the open expanse of the Plains. Texas cattle were driven up the Shawnee Trail to markets in Missouri and Illinois. The Platte River in Nebraska became a highway for immigrants on their way to Oregon, Utah, and California.

Dodge City Reenactors—American Federation of Old West Reenactors (AFOWR) members portray early Dodge City residents at Boot Hill Museum, Dodge City, Kansas.

The Santa Fe Trail burst with activity as merchants supplied new American garrisons in the Southwest and returned with raw products of wool and hides from the newly acquired lands.

This influx of whites did not escape the notice of the Plains Indians. They struck back at intruders with a vengeance. The government established a string of forts and garrisons to help protect the trails. Fort Riley, Fort Larned, Fort Lyon, and Fort Union were just a few of the outposts built to protect valuable commerce along the Santa Fe. The territories of Kansas and Nebraska became hotbeds of conflict as the advancement of white civilization directly countered the north-south migration of the bison herds and the Indians.

Short, violent encounters raged through the Plains. More and more, the Native American found himself crowded, abused, and deceived. The great corridor of Indian domination had been cut in half by the trails of the whites. Rich river bottoms that had provided game and resources were denied and the tribes were forced into the regions of Dakota and Oklahoma.

The tribes received a six-year reprieve of sorts in the 1860s as the Civil War raged in the East. Small, undermanned garrisons of soldiers labored to keep the trails open as the war drained the West of most of its manpower. But with the end of the conflict, an even greater tide of whites intruded on the Indian lands.

The railroads began their steady advance across the Plains. To pay for these roads of steel, the whites encouraged more settlement, creating a greater demand on the natural resources. Cash-poor Texans pushed thousands of cattle toward the railways crossing the tribal lands on the Chisholm, Western, and Goodnight-Loving Trails.

The railroads also brought commercial hunters with an unquenchable thirst for the products of the bison. In less than ten years, from 1865 to 1873, the enormous southern herd was obliterated. The single-resource economy of the Indian collapsed. Starvation and disease defeated a people where gunpowder and bullets had failed. As he watched his way of life crumble before him, the Indian took desperate reprisals. A stone age civilization struggled against an efficient killing machine developed and tempered by the

Ellsworth Reenactors—Members of the Kansas Cowboy Association portray frontier trail life at Ellsworth, Kansas.

Wild Bill—Former AFOWR president, Chris Ball, reenacts William Butler Hickok, one of the most famous of the plainsmen.

Civil War. Muzzle-loading weapons were replaced by cartridge-firing single-shot and repeating rifles.

Even when the Indians had a great numerical advantage, such as in the battle of Beecher's Island, Colorado, they could not overcome the technological advantage of the whites. Fifty men armed with Spencer repeating rifles withstood a determined assault from 600 Cheyenne. Although the soldiers suffered heavy losses, the advantage of the war surplus Spencer carbines saved them from annihilation.

The Indians managed to win a few stunning victories in engagements fought at Fort Phil Kearny and on the Little Big Horn, but they were flukes. Overconfidence and poor leadership defeated the whites on both occasions. The Native American was subdued much as the Confederacy had been defeated. No matter how brilliantly the Indian fought, a few wins meant little. He found himself slowly worn down in a grinding war of attrition by a technological and industrial giant.

End of an Era

By the middle of the 1870s, the Plains were forever altered. The great heads of bison were gone except in the far northern regions. With the herds went the Indian's only hope of independence. Settlements were spreading throughout the grasslands in locations that were once only ruled by the wind. The Santa Fe Trail was abandoned in favor of the advancing railroads. Church bells, telegraph lines, and plows were symbols of new influences upon the land.

It had been a glorious fifty years of struggle, sacrifice, and heroism, but the industrial giant was marching on. The era of the black powder plainsman was fading into history.

3

Traders, Soldiers, and Hunters

TO BEGIN TO UNDERSTAND THE TYPES OF MEN AND WOMEN WHO lived on the Plains during this period a person needs to step back in time. Much knowledge can be gained from reading and study, but it is through living history experiences that a real insight into the lives of these people can be best gained. It has been said that a person only remembers a small proportion of what is read but a large proportion of what is done. Living history and reenactment are exercises in doing that forever alters a person's perception of the lives and conditions of past times.

Bent's Old Fort National Historic Site

One of the best places to get this feel for Plains history is Bent's Old Fort national historic site near La Junta, Colorado. Sitting on the edge of a small rise overlooking the flood plain of the Arkansas River, the fort is truly imposing. It is a walled adobe structure, reconstructed as accurately as possi-

Multipurpose Oxen—Oxen were nothing more than mature steers, usually eaten after a life of toil. Slower than horses for short trips, they made better time than horse teams on long treks. *(Courtesy Santa Fe Trail Center)*

Plains Merchant—Don Hill portrays William Bent at Bent's Old Fort, Colorado. Hill is exhibiting the importance of "proper" period dress while conducting business.

ble to reflect the original in 1845–46. The Arkansas River meanders by the fort about a quarter of a mile south on a course east to the Mississippi. Founded by Bent, St. Vrain & Company in the 1830s, it was an important trade center at the northwest loop of the Santa Fe Trail. The fort reached its zenith as a trade center after the shining times of the Rocky Mountain beaver era. Commerce was centered around the early buffalo hide trade, when Indians and hunters brought in the robes to barter for supplies and luxuries. Horse trading as well as the beaver pelt trade were important elements of the business. The fort did not have to repel an Indian attack. No Indian in his right mind would have taken on such a well-fortified structure unless provoked. William and Charles Bent were on good terms with the natives throughout the post's existence.

Several times a year the National Park Service stages a gathering of living history reenactors to demonstrate the fort's lifestyle. Upon entering the post during an encampment, visitors step back into time. The fort's courtyard is usually full of participants in period dress often outnumbering the visitors. This is not a rendezvous type of gathering but rather a full blown recreation of 1840s life.

Besides buck skinners and Indians, one sees soldiers, businessmen, mule skinners, laborers, and several women in formal and work dress. Reenactors have had to document every tool, article of clothing, and weapon that they wear or use. Reenactments of horse packing, cooking, equipment maintenance, trading, inventory taking, and construction methods keep the visitors occupied throughout the nine hours that the site is open to the public each day. There are also re-creations of Indian dwellings and primitive campsites set up in the cottonwood grove along the river.

The building is constructed almost entirely of adobe as was the fashion of the times. Adobe is a sun-baked clay brick that contains a heavy mix of straw to bind the ingredients. The alternative was sod, which is bricks composed of raw dirt with a top layer of grass to provide a similar binding agent as straw in adobe brick. Adobe and straw possess excellent insulation properties. Most interiors are cool and moist in the summer and warm in the winter. Glass was rare and expensive, so most windows have wooden shutter doors that open to help with ventilation but are closed tight to repel cold weather or hostiles. This fort is no exception. The main gates are the only outward-facing opening and all windows open to the interior of the central square of the fort. The front and side entrances are barred by imposing wooden gates. Adobe walls are up to six feet thick. The gates were the most vulnerable to attack. A small brass cannon protects each gate and was used to fire shot charges of old nails, iron scraps, and rocks.

Indians seldom attacked fortifications of any kind. They preferred to engage an enemy in the open where they could exercise advantages of mobility and speed. There was safety in numbers for whites and Indians alike. A small window for trading with the natives is set to the side of the main gate. Indians were seldom allowed inside the walls of the fort.

Plains Warfare

Most whites did not engage in a running fight with Indians because of the nature of the muzzle-loading Plains rifle. They preferred to make a stand and rely on the superior range and power of their rifles over the bows, spears, and occasional fusils of the enemy. Their stand and fight tactic as opposed to the Indian hit and run tactics was often the deciding factor of Plains skirmishes. If the Indian could hit an enemy hard and quickly enough to force panic, he would win. But if the frontiersman could force a standoff and keep the enemy at a distance, he could force a withdrawal. It sounds simple but it wasn't. Neither side was stupid and rarely engaged in foolish charges. So-called search and destroy tactics are not unique to the Vietnam conflict. These tactics were employed throughout the American Indian Wars by excellent commanders on both sides.

Another common Indian tactic before the advent of repeating rifles was to feint a charge and try to get enough of the whites to fire their rifles to leave them vulnerable. The mounted warriors could then swoop down upon the defenders before they could reload their muzzleloaders. The whites would then be overwhelmed in close combat. The tactic often worked against undisciplined defenders or when numbers were greatly in the Indians' favor.

Sioux Reenactor—Tim Schultz portrays a member of the Mato band of the Sioux nation. Native American reenactment is difficult and demands much time, research, and expense.

The classic defense of Nelson Story's cattle herd against hostiles on the first major cattle drive into Montana is a good example. Story had recently purchased new fast-firing Remington Rolling Block rifles for his cowboys. The Indians had not encountered such rifles before and feigned a charge to draw fire. Story believed that his small force would have been overwhelmed had they been armed with single-shot muzzleloaders. This is the reason why the six-shot percussion Colt revolver was a popular backup weapon to the muzzle-loading rifle. Previously, the Colt men often carried at least two single-shot pistols to back up a rifle.

A Different World

One of the first things a modern-day visitor would notice if he could step back in time to visit a place like Bent's Old Fort would have been the odors. The visitor would be bombarded with the odors of horses, cattle, green hides, open latrines, compost, and unwashed bodies. There would be sights that are rarely seen today. Back injuries, broken arms and legs, eye problems, and an assortment of other ailments were left largely to nature to heal as best as it could. Medical practice of that day was composed mainly to cut it off, cut it out, or burn it. The use of harsh purgatives to get an infection out of the system was a popular form of cure. Bleeding, blistering, and amputations were attempted for everything from colds to infections. The phrase "kill him or cure him" was often literally the case in frontier medicine.

One early journal tells of soldiers in Stephen Kearny's invasion of the Southwest during the Mexican War. These men were so afraid of the medical officer and his cures that they hid from him during bouts of fever. When they had recovered

Indian Trade Musket—The most enduring muzzleloader on the Plains was the Indian trade musket. A primitive action and flintlock ignition system was relatively easy to repair in uncivilized areas. The gun was still sold in Canada in the early 20th century.

enough to hide the condition, they rejoined the unit. Bad teeth were commonplace. Most people habitually covered their mouths when near strangers. It is the reason why toothy smiles are seldom seen in period photographs.

Clothing was heavy and full length to keep the body as fully covered as possible. The less that was exposed to the elements, the less a frontiersman would need to use valuable water to wash. I have seen period coat collars that were covered with grime to the point that the grease and dirt were caked and cracked like old vinyl. Shirts were considered underwear and neither men nor women considered it proper dress to go about in shirt sleeves without an overgarment. This explains why shirts had no pockets. Men wore belts to carry their tools but they kept their pants up with suspenders. It was considered unhealthy to tightly bind the waist. As far as toilet paper and feminine hygienic care were concerned, they did the best they could with what they had. Most people used their hands to wipe and then washed or wiped off the hand.

Lice, fleas, and bed bugs were a constant nemesis. More than a few people died from infections from rat bites. A big reason that Indians and certain whites were not allowed in the post was the visitors that they carried on their bodies which were just as deadly and unpleasant as the people themselves. Sickness and contamination killed far more Indians and whites than the fiercest battles. The average lifespan was forty years. It wasn't unusual for a couple to lose half of their children before they were grown. Most marriages averaged only seven years. Widows, widowers, and orphans were very common. Blended families composed of several half brothers, half sisters, adopted children, cousins, and stepparents were the norm.

People were generally religious and believed in a God who punished on this earth. All one needed to do was look around at all the misery being dealt out to these poor dregs of humanity for confirmation of such a belief. Superstition influenced many decisions. This was a tough, cruel world being administered by tough and often cruel people. Justice was handed out swiftly and

1840s Soldier—Jim Bemen in a dragoon outfit of the 1840s with summer top and dark campaign pants. Yellow strips indicate officer status.

surely by those in control, often because there was no place to keep a prisoner. Thieves were hung because thievery could kill. Life on the Plains was both precious and cheap. It just depended on whose life it was.

Men and Women

It was the young men who ventured onto the Plains. White women were very seldom seen and much appreciated when they were. If a man took a wife, she was usually either Indian or Mexican. A good wife demanded a high price no matter what her race. The larger the family, the larger the labor pool and the greater the chances for survival and prosperity. A man appreciated a healthy woman who could provide many children. A large, healthy woman was preferred to one of slight build. Few men could afford the burden of a sickly woman.

Three basic trades flourished on the Plains frontier society. This was a time of cheap labor and expensive goods. To work for someone else often meant a life of poverty so most people tried to function as independent contractors of some sort. The trader provided goods and services for large profits. The risks were great so the profits had to be great. The hunter and trapper was a supplier of raw materials. His return had to be large to justify his being out there in the first place.

Why a man would want to be a soldier seems far more complex. The enlisted man was subjected to low pay, harsh discipline, unhealthy environments, and some measure of danger. He did have the security of having someone to tell him what to do. For the young man there was a real sense of adventure. The officer could use his position as a stepping stone to greater things but the common soldier had little to look forward to. It is a small wonder that many companies were made up of recent immigrants who were unable to find work elsewhere.

Often, especially on the Plains, companies were raised for very short periods of enlistment. Usually these volunteer regiments were formed as a temporary solution to the constant problem of Indian relations. Since there was a shortage of manpower, one can image the type of riffraff that usually joined these volunteer companies. The early Texas Rangers were organized in a similar fashion, especially for campaigns against the Comanche and other hostile tribes. Makeshift as it was, the system worked fairly well and lasted into the 1870s.

Bent's Old Fort was not a military post, but it was used by Stephen Kearny's forces on their trek to take control of New Mexico and California during the war with Mexico. The Bents had some financial troubles later because the government refused to recognize much of the brothers' expenses for billeting the troops during their stay.

As one might guess, formal education was of little importance. Most trades and skills were learned under some sort of apprentice system. When someone did have a good education, he usually could rise to leadership positions quickly. Even Kit

Carson, who achieved high rank in the army after his mountain man days, could do little more than sign his name. Contracts and other business negotiations were conducted by word of mouth and a handshake. Problems arose when the government demanded that contracts be written before they were honored. This was part of the Bents' difficulties with receiving payment for Kearny's troops. When there was a disagreement, it sometimes led to violence. If a man was unwilling to stand up for his rights, then this was not the place for him. Most of these people were of frontier heritage and taking the law into their own hands was the accepted method if there was no formal law available. The Bents were the law at Bent's Fort. Whether or not a trader or his post survived depended in large part upon his fairness and how it was perceived by all elements of society. The Bents were highly successful and there are several examples of their innate good judgment.

A World of Nobility and Ignorance

It was a world of nobility as well as ignorance and danger. It was a world where life could be both cheap and cherished at the same time. Justice, legality, right, and wrong were often the result of local concepts and conditions. Men used all of their skills and intelligence to survive. In some ways it was a world to be envied, but for the most part it would have been a very uncomfortable and dark existence for those who dwell in this modern world that is its legacy.

4

Black Powder Guns of the Plains

CHOOSING A BLACK POWDER WEAPON FROM TODAY'S MARKET IS a gun lover's dream. Choices of pistols, revolvers, and rifles are numerous, and a shooter today can have almost anything that is desired. For the most part, prices are extremely moderate considering the quality of the products. One's choice may be dictated by price and availability. Catalogs can be obtained from each of the firms marketing black powder arms and the buyer shouldn't hesitate to order from any of these companies if the products aren't available locally. The Internet has opened up a whole new marketplace for black powder arms location and procurement. Addresses for many of the firms are listed in the last chapter of this book. The buyer should take his time, critically examine the options, and be certain of choices. This tactic provides more satisfaction in the long run.

The Flintlock—The flintlock plains rifle was used on the Plains from the late 1700s until the end of the American Indian Wars. Flint and steel ignition systems, were easy for the Indian to maintain. Often while a more modern weapon was saved for battle, the flintlock was the everyday hunting rifle of the Native American.

Replica Arms

There are several replica arms which are suitable for reenactment. If a reenactor is particularly fussy he may desire an original weapon. He should be prepared to experience a large dent in the pocketbook. As black powder interest continues to grow, these old weapons have skyrocketed in value. Most of us make do with replicas, especially if we want to shoot them. Kits are available from most manufacturers. Kits allow the enthusiast to finish a weapon with an antique finish. Many appear extremely authentic. This can become a challenging hobby. Most of the weapons that will be mentioned will usually pass inspection right out of the box.

Lyman Products of Middlefield, Connecticut markets its Great Plains Rifle and Trade Rifle in percussion and flintlock. Although Lyman doesn't offer as wide a selection as others, what they do offer is of excellent quality and is very authentic.

Uberti USA Inc. of Lakeville, Connecticut produces a Hawken Santa Fe in percussion and flintlock which is superb. Navy Arms of Ridgefield, New Jersey, offers a wide variety of excellent replicas covering the entire period of the plainsman. I might add that their long rifles do not have the stock divided to save costs. Many firms have gone to this on full-stock models but Navy keeps the wood in one piece all the way to the end of the muzzle. This makes for a much more beautiful and authentic piece. Navy and Dixie Gun Works offer a wide variety of Civil War replicas as well as fine target models. Connecticut Valley Arms (CVA), an importer based in Norcross, Georgia, markets a nice Mountain rifle was well as a Civil War Zouave replica. Traditions Inc. of Old Saybrook, Connecticut, offers one of the most complete lines of replica muzzle-loading and cartridge arms. Many of them are approved for reenactment activities.

Almost any Civil War replica will work for post–Civil War reenactment on the Plains. After the war, surplus military rifles and pistols were common. Several arms manufacturing firms went out of business because they couldn't compete against the massive numbers of cheap, war surplus arms being dumped on the market. Zouaves, Springfields, and Spencers were highly prized and made up a large part of the early bison hunting arms, especially when the weapons could be bought for literally pennies. For years these war surplus weapons were the arms of the common man in the West. It is interesting to note that the largest purchaser of surplus Spencer repeating carbines after the war was Oliver Winchester. He recognized the threat that these surplus Spencers presented against the sales of his new and pricey Model 1866 Winchester repeater. Most of the Spencers were destroyed.

Modern Hunting Muzzleloaders

The thin line separating the historical replicas from the more modern option is in many cases the sights. Since so much of the share of the market is for big game hunting, modern sights are demanded by the buyer. Recoil pads are also placed on many models. Barrel lengths have been shortened because modern black powder and Pyrodex are so much more efficient that the powders of the 19th century. This more modern type, which I classify as a replica hunter, is the largest offering that the muzzleloader shooter has to choose from.

Thompson/Center of Rochester, New Hampshire, is a sales leader for the hunting share of the market. Their sidelocks are designed for shooting dependability and convenience and not particularly concerned with absolute historical accuracy. They are modern designs that look the part of old-time muzzleloaders. Most Thompson/Center sidelocks have faster rates of twist to the rifling to better accommodate the use of Minie balls and bullets. Over the years Thompson/Center has marketed the Hawken, Renegade, Cherokee, and New Englander models. The Pennsylvania Hunter flintlock had a 1:60" twist for shooting round balls. A .58 caliber rifle called the Big Boar was a popular Thompson/Center model for several years.

Without a doubt the leader in replica arms production is Davide Pedersoli & Co. of Brescia, Italy. For over fifty years, Pedersoli has been producing guns that faithfully duplicate models of the American tradition. Reproductions of military and civilian models of the period represent both the culture and the history of the American frontier. Ultramodern manufacturing techniques and equipment have made Pedersoli replicas highly accurate and affordable. Pedersoli replicas are marketed by a number of companies and distributors in the United States.

The Modern In-Line—The In-Line rifle, such as this Traditions Kodiak, is used by modern-day hunters and is far different from the early Plains rifles.

Navy Arms Buffalo Hunter—The Navy Arms Buffalo Hunter is a Civil War replica that has been redesigned to act as a modern hunting rifle. This .58 caliber carbine uses a musket cap ignition and is a superior short to medium-range hunting rifle.

Cabela's Hawken Hunter Carbine—The Cabela's Hawken Hunter Carbine is a modern sidelock replica hunter. This .54 caliber carbine has modern hunting sights, a rubber recoil pad, and sling studs not found on historic replicas. While this .54 caliber carbine won't do for reenactment, it is a fine hunting muzzleloader.

Modern Replica Hunter—This is the author's custom English Sporting Rifle made by Doctor Gary White. In spite of laminated stock, black ice metal finish, modern Williams sights, and rubber recoil pad, the rifle easily fits within all United States muzzleloader-only hunting regulations yet performs like a modern in-line.

Traditions Crockett—The Traditions Crockett is a fine example of a replica suitable for reenactment that still functions very well as a modern muzzle-loading hunting arm.

Traditions also designs most of its line to appeal to modern hunters. Woodsman, Hunter, Frontier, and Trapper models are equipped with modern sights. The Crockett .32 caliber rifle is an excellent replica. My first new muzzleloader was a Traditions Hawken Hunter. Besides being a beautiful rifle, it was dependable and accurate. I carried it for eight years and shot everything from jackrabbits to coyotes to mule deer. It never failed to provide outstanding performance.

CVA and Navy also offer a wide variety of modern sidelock muzzleloaders. Navy offered a Mule Ear percussion for several years called the Country Boy. All of these modern sidelocks have the general look of original rifles but generally are not acceptable for reenactment.

On many sidelocks, a set trigger option is available. In a set trigger configuration there is one trigger that is used to set or make the second trigger a hair trigger. This option greatly enhances accuracy and doesn't take much practice to master. I have two hunting and reenactment sidelocks custom-made by Dr. Gary White of Roosevelt, Utah. One is a .50 caliber English Sporting Rifle replica and the other is a .58 caliber Leman Plains Rifle replica. Both have set triggers and are excellent hunters. While the Sporting rifle is not suitable for reenactment it will rival any modern or replica muzzleloader on the market. The Leman is perfectly suited for post-1820 reenactment and I use it often. Both are excellent hunters.

There are also some fine inexpensive youth models offered by CVA, Navy, and Traditions that are proportioned for the small-frame shooter. Stock fit is important for developing a youngster's confidence and ability. Length of pull refers to the distance from the butt of the rifle to the trigger. If it is too long the shooter is thrown off balance and cannot sight the rifle properly. Recoil is also a problem if the stock is too long. Heavy recoil can ruin a potential shooter's confidence and cause overcompensation to the pounding that is experienced. Youth models can be purchased for about the same price as an average-quality .22 rimfire rifle. The trend toward modernization in muzzle-loading goes beyond the outward appearance of old-time sidelocks. There are hunters who couldn't care less about traditional appearance but demand a rifle that is as modern as possible in both design and look. Several companies have sidelock offerings to meet that trend.

The Lyman Deerstalker features a rubber recoil pad, coil springs rather than flat springs in the firing mechanism, and a fine receiver sight blended into a more conventional style. Traditions has a Trophy model and a Pioneer model that feature pistol grip wrists, recoil pads, sling swivels, and synthetic ramrods.

The In-Line Muzzleloader

Beginning in the late 1980s with the introduction of the Knight MK-85, the in-line muzzleloader came upon the North American hunting scene. The in-line was created so hunters could take advantage of special muzzle-loading seasons and

Muzzleloader Battery—Both modern in-line and historical replica make up the author's muzzleloader battery. The guns range from primitive round ball design to the ultramodern muzzleloader. From the top is a .58 caliber Leman Plains Rifle replica, a 12 gauge Cabela's double-barrel shotgun, a Traditions in-line muzzleloader shotgun with red dot sights, and a Traditions Pursuit Pro in-line .50 caliber rifle with Traditions 3-9X scope.

carry a rifle of modern design. The in-line became very popular and represents over eighty percent of new muzzleloader sales. All of the major companies and many new ones got into the in-line muzzleloader market.

Each year new models came out and new in-line systems were introduced. Original in-lines were open striker designs firing a #11 percussion cap. The development of plastic sabots to contain jacketed pistol bullets and pellet style propellants brought about more changes and enhancements. Bolt action, drop action, and break action rifles crowded the market. The 209 shotgun primer and sulfur free propellants continued the trend toward a muzzleloader that was far removed from the original intent of the special muzzleloader only season.

At one time there were over a dozen major companies marketing in-line muzzleloaders. Today there are only five major and a few small companies still producing in-lines. In the competitive spirit of capitalism, rifle performance claims became more and more outlandish until the whole credibility of the in-line industry was in question. Several states have removed in-lines, pellet propellants, and sabot projectiles from their muzzleloader-only hunting seasons. This trend will continue if performance claims continue to misrepresent the true capability of a muzzleloader.

My custom sidelock English Sporting Rifle will perform with any in-line ever manufactured because its barrel rifling twist really makes the difference in what a muzzleloader will shoot effectively. No in-line is suitable for reenactment or historical events.

Cartridge Firearms

During the Civil War, a new trend in rifles was perfected that would eventually end the reign of the muzzleloader as the frontiersman's primary firearm. Self-contained cartridge-firing rifles began their rise to domination. Historically accurate for a Plains reenactment or suitable for hunting is the Henry repeating lever action rifle. Over 13,000 saw service during the Civil War. The greatest drawback to these rifles was the weak, unreliable .44 rimfire cartridge that the rifle used. It kept the Winchester from being seriously considered for hunting big game of the period. Today's beautiful replicas are offered in several handgun calibers rather than the discontinued original rimfire. Rounds such as .45 Colt and .44-40 make these replicas serious medicine for short-range deer hunting. Navy, Uberti, and EMF, as well as others, sell lever action replicas. Navy has steel- and brass-framed Henrys. The later 1866 Winchester is also available. This model features a wooden forearm and side gate loading that did not exist on the Henry.

The lever action did not reign as king of the plains rifles for several years after its introduction. There was a considerable length of time during and after the Civil War when the single shot breech loading cartridge rifle was considered the best

Trapdoor Springfield—The most common cartridge rifle on the Plains after the Civil War was the Trapdoor Springfield, a conversion from a Civil War muzzleloader. This was the carbine carried by cavalry troopers. (*Courtesy Traditions Inc.)*

Sharps Long Range—The most legendary of the Plains rifles is the Sharps. This is the often glamorized single shot buffalo rifle. *(Courtesy Traditions Inc.)*

1860 Henry—Originally manufactured by Volcanic Arms Company during the Civil War, the Henry was chambered for the neither dependable nor powerful .44 Henry Flat rimfire cartridge. *(Courtesy Traditions Inc.)*

1866 Winchester—After Volcanic Arms took bankruptcy, one of the stockholders, shirt manufacturer Oliver Winchester, took over the company and significantly improved the rifle. This is the famous "Yellow Boy" rifle. *(Courtesy Traditions Inc.)*

1873 Winchester—The repeating rifle that toppled the single shot from its reign of dominance was the Model 1873 Winchester which was chambered for the .44-40 centerfire round. *(Courtesy Traditions Inc.)*

Remington Rolling Block—This wonderfully sturdy rifle exceeded the Sharps in both civilian and military sales. This was the rifle Custer carried in the Battle of the Little Big Horn. *(Courtesy Traditions Inc.)*

that a man could buy. The Winchester didn't have a reliable, powerful round capable of handling bison, bears, and other large game. Breech loaders were more powerful and dependable. Many of the bison rifles were Remington Rolling Blocks, Trapdoor Springfield rifles, a few Spencers, and Sharps drop block rifles. The Sharps is the most glamorous of the bison rifles but the Remington outsold it and the most common breech loader of the period was the Trapdoor Springfield.

Traditions, Navy, Dixie, Taylor, and others market replica Sharps, Remingtons, and Springfield rifles. Normally these rifles are chambered for the .45-70 Government cartridge and are capable of taking any game in North America. I have owned and hunted with replicas of all three. I currently own a Sharps replica because my reenactment character, Jonah William Campbell, preferred a Sharps. All of them functioned very well and proved to be excellent hunting rifles.

Shiloh Rifle Company of Big Timber, Montana, offers a wide selection of superior quality Sharps replicas. C. Sharps Arms also markets a replica of the 1874 Sharps. Both companies offer a wide choice of custom caliber and appearance

Percussion Plain Pistol—This single shot muzzleloader was commonly carried on the Plains from 1820 until 1860. Powerful and dependable, it was the close range backup for the Plains rifle. *(Courtesy Traditions Inc.)*

1851 Navy—When Colt's .36 caliber, six-shot, percussion revolver came on the market, it sold by the thousands. The Navy Colt was well balanced, powerful, and accurate. It was carried throughout the remainder of the 19th century. *(Courtesy Traditions Inc.)*

offerings. These are probably better rifles than the originals and are the supreme expression of the gunmaker's art for this style of rifle.

Black Powder Pistols

Black powder pistols are probably the most popular type of muzzle-loading arms. Except for the Paterson replica, revolvers came too late for the mountain man period but worked perfectly for the Plains period after 1846. Percussion revolvers today are accurate, well made, and economical. Most follow the Colt or Remington designs but there are several other available replica revolvers.

Navy Arms and Traditions market everything from the Paterson and Walker Colts to the Confederate models. I have owned and written about literally all of the percussion revolvers. My favorite is the Model 1860 Colt Army because of its

1858 Remington—This was Colt's number one competitor during the Civil War. People complained that it tended to "get out of works" from black powder contamination in an extended fire fight. *(Courtesy Traditions Inc.)*

1860 Colt Army—The premier percussion revolver of the Civil War, it was produced until 1873, when it was replaced by the 1873 Army cartridge revolver. *(Courtesy Traditions Inc.)*

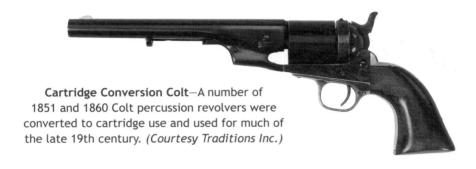

Cartridge Conversion Colt—A number of 1851 and 1860 Colt percussion revolvers were converted to cartridge use and used for much of the late 19th century. *(Courtesy Traditions Inc.)*

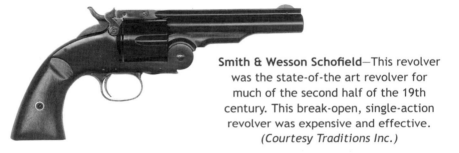

Smith & Wesson Schofield—This revolver was the state-of-the art revolver for much of the second half of the 19th century. This break-open, single-action revolver was expensive and effective. *(Courtesy Traditions Inc.)*

balance. Unlike so many handguns of the period, the Model 1860 just feels good in the shooter's hand. It has a balance and grace that has never been equaled in any handgun. Modern replicas feature all of these qualities.

I carried a Navy Arms replica of a Griswald and Gunnison 1851 Colt copy made by the Confederates during the Civil War. It was my number one sidearm for years. It was .36 caliber and an excellent shooter. Replicas of the Spiller and Burr, the Rogers and Spencer, and even the fantastic Le Mat combination revolver are offered by companies. Uberti brand replicas are considered to be the finest and will usually bring higher prices.

Many of the Confederate replicas and some Colt and Remington replicas have brass rather than steel frames. For the same reason that they were originally manufactured, brass-framed revolvers are less expensive than steel framed revolvers. You may read that the brass-framed revolvers are not guaranteed as well because they will eventually shoot loose under heavy loads. I have put hundreds of moderate 28-grain propellant charged rounds through brass-framed revolvers and never experienced any problems. While steel frames are stronger, it is difficult to wear a brass-framed revolver out if you take care of it. I would not hesitate to carry a brass-framed revolver for normal hunting, plinking, and reenactment activities.

5

Reenactment— How to Begin

FOR MANY, A NATURAL OUTGROWTH OF MUZZLE-LOADING interest is taking part in living history reenactment. Although I have never considered myself to be a particularly craftsy person, I found myself being drawn into this interesting aspect of the hobby. As I became more involved, I began attending living history demonstrations and paying particular attention to outfits, styles, and tools being used in paintings and photos of the period. Before long, I found myself putting on a primitive outfit as much to satisfy my curiosity as anything else.

Reenactment on a Budget

I am more than aware of what it means to work with a limited budget. It is not uncommon for a total investment in an historical outfit to exceed $1,000. Many reenactors spend years researching and putting together their outfits and have invested many times that figure. By the same token, one shouldn't convince himself that reenactment is a rich man's hobby out of reach of the working man. Some people may drive a Cadillac but most get by with a lot less and still manage to reach their destination.

The same principle applies when putting together an outfit. I am well aware of those fortunate few who can purchase a fancy, custom-made, brain-tanned suit of clothes and can easily afford a custom-made firearm. It is very impressive. For many, an expenditure of $60 or $100 a month toward this hobby can be tough and at first calls for some will power. Bringing in an outfit on a tight budget is possible and can, over a few short months, produce some fine results.

The author's original plains reenactment outfit: a muslin shirt using a pattern from the *Book of Buskskinning IV*, drop-front pants, cloth suspenders, leather botas, and moccasins from Tandy Pattern.

My first suggestion for the beginner is to start reading. Begin your research before you begin your outfit. As you work your way through books, magazine, and photos, one of the primary things you should notice is that all buckskinners do not have to wear buckskins. Lots of folks back then were dressed in fabrics.

In today's market, fabrics are much cheaper than leather. Unbleached muslin can be bought for pennies down at the local Walmart as can flannel and serge. If you are willing to learn to sew then it is fairly easy to put together a modest outfit. Sometimes cheap leather can be found at garage sales and auctions. Worn ladies' and men's leather clothing can often be purchased quite reasonably and taken apart to make leather accessories. Using a simple grocery sack pattern that you have cut out and shaped into whatever you want to make will save money, provides hours of entertain-

ment, and produce some surprisingly authentic goods. Don't worry if your first attempts look crude. That crude work can often provide a great deal of authenticity and gives outfits some badly needed character.

Zippers, polyester, fake suede, riveted blue jeans, canvas shoes, composition soles, plastic, and vinyl didn't exist no matter how authentic one might think he can make it appear. Most corduroy is acceptable as long as it is the old time wide rib type.

Decide on a character and work toward that goal. Develop a concept

The same outfit for cooler weather with the additions of an overshirt made from the same pattern and heavier serge material.

For cold weather, an inexpensive capote is worn over the other shirts and provides surprising warmth.

of his or her image from photos, drawings, and descriptions of the period and then re-create the dress as best you can. By going this route you can be sure of historical accuracy. Be certain that the date and location of the image is right. Movies are a poor source. The time may come when you will need to document your outfit to be able to take part in a particular event and Robert Redford dressed as Jeremiah Johnson just won't work. Forget about the philosophy of reenactment that is proposed by some which states, "If it had existed, they would have used it." Just because something existed doesn't automatically mean that it would have been usable or within the budget of the common man. Use common sense and you will probably do well.

Standard Dress and Equipment on the Plains

Standard dress on the Plains followed certain patterns. The universal weaponry, especially among freighters and travelers on the trails, was the rifle, handgun, and what the old-timers called a Bowie knife. The term Bowie knife was generic for almost anything from a large butcher or skinning knife to the more traditionally styled Bowie that we are familiar with today. These knives were probably carried in conjunction with smaller knives used for different chores. When one is around

In extreme cold, the capote's hood keeps the ears warm and the head covered.

Warm Weather Outfit—John Harrington in a good outfit of the Plains. Note the Tegras mocs and leather botas which would be worn in all weather conditions.

any percussion or flintlock firearms for long, the importance of these large knives for self-defense becomes evident. Even later-period percussion revolvers are not dependable when compared to modern-day firearms. Add the elements of wear and tear plus weather extremes encountered on the Plains and anyone can easily imagine why a large knife would be so important as a backup weapon. Men involved with driving teams or cracking oxen down those lonely trails could not safely tolerate the distraction of fumbling with a large rifle throughout the day. Unless a man was mounted, which most teamsters were not, the rifle was kept within easy reach at the front of the wagon. A belt pistol and large knife were a much more practical solution for quick defense. Many could not afford a pistol. After the advent of the percussion revolver, Colts became standard issue. Russell, Majors and Waddell, a famous freighting company on the trails, issued two Colt revolvers as well as a bible to each employee. This is why their teamsters were almost universally called "bible backs."

The era just preceding the Civil War, 1830–1860, was the time of the Plains rifle. A short, powerful rifle of .50 to .58 caliber, it had little ornamentation. It was a simple, practical percussion rifle with a maximum range of two hundred yards. If under attack, whites would fort up and try to keep Indians at a distance using the rifle's

Merchant's Outfit—Bill Brown in a merchant's outfit of the 1830-50 period. The remnant of a cutaway coat is made of denim and is an artifact of this period.

Bookkeeper's Outfit— The bookkeeper of a Santa Fe trading expedition relaxes in camp. Note the wire-rimmed glasses and straw hat.

superior range. This same principle is the reason for the army's adoption of the Trapdoor Springfield as it cartridge arm after the Civil War.

The Indians favored a fusil in the early years when they could get a firearm. It was a cheap, heavy, smooth bore .60 to .70 caliber flintlock, commonly called the Indian Trade Musket today. The Indian used it mostly for bison hunting, which for him was a short-range encounter from the back of a running pony. Fumbling with a patched ball from the back of a running horse was difficult. The Indian rode into a herd with a mouthful of lead balls. After a shot, usually no more than two feet from his target, he poured powder down the barrel, spit a loose fitting ball into the bore, and struck the butt of the rifle on the ground. With the flash hole slightly bored out, this hard thump on the ground tended to prime the flash pan of the gun.

All that was left for him to do was to cock his piece and deliver another shot to his next victim. This technique gave him what was probably the fastest firing single shot on the plains. But because of the nature of the loose-fitting, smooth bore musket, it limited his effective range to only sixty or seventy yards. The white man wanted to keep the Indian beyond seventy yards. Most early Plains Indians, however, were armed with bows and lances which kept their effective fighting distance limited.

Civilian's Outfit—Bill Gwaltney in a civilian form of the military cap. This was popular dress for several years.

Bent, St. Vrain Merchants—Jack Wise (left) and Jerry Hays of the Bent, St. Vrain Company in the Bent's Old Fort Store. Jack's paper would have been popular entertainment in the West, especially if someone was available to read it aloud.

Doctor or Lawyer's Outfit— Heavy clothing such as this was popular during the early 1800s.

Plains Clothing

Boots were important to the plainsman. Protecting feet became very important when these men spent as much time on foot as they did. Boots were low-heeled with heavy soles. They tended to be at least calf high, and lace-up boots were not uncommon. Moccasins could be worn by horsemen but were inadequate for teamsters or farmers. Anyone who has had his foot stepped on by a horse or cow would recognize immediately the shortcomings of the moccasin. For reenactment, a pair of Wellington boots is fairly accurate. Modern cowboy boots with stitched patterns on the toe are absolutely unacceptable. They didn't appear until the middle of the 1870s and stitched toe patterns were not present until after the turn of the century.

Heavy woolen or flannel shirts were worn and when the weather turned brisk, men often wore two. Cotton shirts were worn during warm weather. A vest or jacket was almost always standard apparel. Pants were loose fitting, high-waisted and often of drop-front style until the 1850s when the button fly trouser became more popular. Belt loops are a 20th century development and not correct. Denim was commonly worn. Don't allow the Levi legend of the 1849 California gold rush steer you away from denim. Levi Strauss invented the use of rivets to support critical stress points. Denim was used for years before that.

Trail Outfit—Harry Misner in a Santa Fe Trail outfit. The boots are typical of those favored by teamsters.

The Universal Poncho—The poncho was the all-purpose garment for warmth and protection from the elements.

An interesting point about clothing should be made concerning this period. The farmer in the fields and the businessman in town generally wore the same style of clothing. In the 1830s, a cutaway coat and frock vest wore worn pitching hay as well as behind the banker's desk. What differed was the material used to make the clothing. While the businessman might have a suit of wool or linen, the working man wore cotton or flannel. Tailors sewed clothing together, but they often just cut out the patterns and the purchaser or his lady finished the garment. This was a time of cheap labor and expensive goods. Clothes could be elaborately styled, even for the working man, because hand labor held little value. The tailor made his profit from sales of the material, not from sewing the garment together. As a reenactor,

it would logically follow that as long as the material is correct and the style appropriate to the character's lifestyle, almost any pattern of the period will work. Few people dressed like mountain men unless they were forced to by economic conditions. Even though they might be wearing homespun, they kept their clothing up to the current styles.

Hats were also important. Men just didn't go outdoors bareheaded. They needed that protection against the elements. The Plains environment favored the style of the low crowned, brimmed felt hat, but anything that

Billy Dixon—Mark Fergeson as post-Civil War buffalo hunter Billy Dixon.

protected the head was preferable to nothing. Straw hats and many styles of caps were commonly worn. If nothing else was available, then a tightly bound bandana covering the head would serve. Top hats were the height of style and could be frequently found, even if they were made of straw for warm weather.

Fort Worth Policeman—Tom Wiederhold as a Fort Worth policeman of the late 19th century.

Dragoon Sergeant—John Lemon portrays an 1840s era dragoon sergeant in field uniform top and summer weight bottoms. When on campaign the soldier would be dressed in solid blue.

Cavalry Officer—Lt. Colonel Miles Keogh of the 7th Cavalry. Notice the brocade and fancy light blue collar of the coat.

Coats were heavy and long to afford maximum protections. An overshirt of homespun or leather would often work the same as a modern windbreaker. Most were pullover or wraparound in style, little more than extra shirts, especially for work wear.

Leggings or botas were commonly worn by the plainsman. These garments offered important protection to the lower legs. In the brush country of Texas and the Southwest they evolved into the chaps commonly worn by the cowboy and the Mexican *vaquero*. At a time when even a minor scratch could become a serious infection, leggings were essential to the white man as well as the Indian. Indian women did not go without this protective garment. In warm weather, an Indian male might be almost naked but he would be wearing his leggings.

Stockings were worn when they could be had, but underwear was not commonly used. Long underwear became popular just prior to the Civil War. The long-tailed shirt functioned as underwear in those days. In cases of sickness, a man just made do with what he could find. These were gritty times to say the least.

Resources

The following organizations can help you design and obtain the material for a historical outfit. This is by no means a complete list but it provides the beginner with a place to start.

Muzzle Blasts
National Muzzle Loading Rifle Association
P.O. Box 67
Friendship, IN 47021

This is a magazine published by the National Muzzle Loading Rifle Association. You will need to join the Association to get a subscription, but the writing, advice, and advertisements are excellent. I highly recommend joining if your interests center on pre–1850 reenactment.

Muzzleloader
Scurlock Publishing Company
1293 Myrtle Springs Rd.
Texarkana, TX 75503

This is a bimonthly magazine without club affiliation that is an excellent source for pre–1850 reenactment information.

Whispering Wind
P.O. Box 1390 (Dept. 3)
Folsom, LA 70437-1390

This is an important source for Indian crafts, history, and culture.

Blue & Gray Magazine
522 Norton Rd.
Columbus, OH 43228.

Blue & Gray Magazine is a full-color, 68 page, bimonthly Civil War magazine. Each issue features our "General's Tour," an in-depth article by a qualified historian, including a driving tour, illustrated with lots of period and modern-day color photographs, and our highly acclaimed color maps.

The Books of Buckskinning
1293 Myrtle Springs Rd.
Texarkana, TX 75503

This is a series of specialty books that offer everything from patterns to how-to articles that are invaluable for information on dressing for the colonial and mountain man roles.

Dixie Gun Works, Inc.
P.O. Box 130
Gunpowder Lane
Union City, TN 38281

The largest catalog of its kind. Numerous items of clothing, patterns, and many unusual parts are offered by this company. Just reading the catalog is a treat.

Cain's Outdoor
1832 Williams Highway
Williamstown, WV 26187
(304) 375-7842, (800) 445-1776

A good catalog for finding primitive supplies.

Bent, St. Vrain & Company
7235 South Dover Court
Littleton, CO 80128

A good source for Mexican War military uniforms and Bent era goods.

Regimental Quartermaster
3069 Edison Furlong Rd.
Furlong, PA 18925

Civil War–era reenactment clothing and supplies

Tandy Leather Company Inc.
3847 East Loop 820 South
Fort Worth , TX 76119

Leathers, patterns, skins, and trimmings are available through an excellent catalog if you don't have a local store.

Fall Creek Suttlery
P.O. Box 92
Whitestown, IN 46075

A good organization for finding later period goods and accouterments of the Civil War period.

La Pelleterie
P.O. Box 127, Highway 41
Arrow Rock, MO 65320

A Missouri outfit with some quality goods, especially for civilian dress.

Carl Dyer
P.O. Box 31, State Road 62
Friendship, IN 47021

A good source of excellent moccasins.

Crazy Crow Trading Post
P.O. Box 847
Pottsboro, TX 75076

Crazy Crow Trading Post is the largest supplier of Native American and American mountain man crafts, craft supplies, and craft kits in the world. An excellent source of reasonably priced goods.

Texas Jacks Wild West Outfitter
117 North Adams Street
Fredericksburg, TX 78624

A good source for Old West clothing and leather goods.

Wild West Mercantile
7302 E. Main Street, Suite 7
Mesa, AZ 85207

Another good source for Old West clothing and leather goods.

Drovers Mercantile
119 North Douglas Avenue
Ellsworth, KS 67439

Source of the Kansas Cowboy Association, drover era clothing and goods, and the excellent *Kansas Cowboy Newspaper*, one of the best sources for drover era information.

Reenactment Guild of America
C/O David Akins
832 ACR 1405
Elkhart, TX 75839
www.rgamerica.org

A new organization dedicated to historically correct 19th century reenactment. Chat online at www.gunfighterzone.com.

Track of the Wolf, Inc.
18308 Joplin Street, NW
Elk River, MN 55330-1773

This company features top-of-the-line custom and antique rifles and shotguns made by some of the finest primitive gunsmiths in the country. If you want the very best, this is the source. They also sell a variety of support equipment, instruction manuals, and accoutrements.

6

The Woman's Role

TO ATTEMPT TO KEEP THE WOMAN'S ROLE ON THE PLAINS COMpletely separate from the role of men would only blur the real situation in most cases. While it is true that women were generally regarded as having only one function, in reality they acted in an enormous variety of situations and conditions throughout the history of the Plains. Whatever responsibility can be described for a man can be found, at one time or another, being filled and performed by women.

Throughout the early period of the Santa Fe Trail, there is very little evidence of white women being present. During the first twenty-five years that the trail was being used, probably fewer than a dozen women crossed it. Most of these travelers were mainly female relatives of Mexican traders traveling east. In 1846, a woman named Susan Magoffin accompanied her husband, Samuel, to New Mexico on business and wrote of her experiences in a journal that claimed her as the first American woman to make the trip. Her description of Bent's Old Fort at that time is probably the best record written. After the War with Mexico, the former Mexican lands of the West and Southwest were open to American settlement and women by the thousands traveled over the Santa Fe, Oregon, and Mormon Trails. The coming of women transformed the Plains.

The Real versus the Myth

To gain a proper prospective of women of the Plains, it is necessary to dispel a number of myths about women at this time that have developed in fictionalized accounts. Plains women were not the frail prairie flowers that many would have

Photographic Evidence—Since we knew that this lady was born in 1826 and appears to be no more than 35 years of age, we can conservatively date this image to the late 1850s. The front buttoning, curved side seam bodice without accentuating the bosom, and full sleeves match 1850s styles.

us imagine. They were tough, hard-working, enterprising, independent settlers who bore every bit as much of the burden of life on the Plains as the men did. In many cases, the women conducted their lives alone and prospered in this rough environment. Women established farms and ranches, functioned in business, fought off Indians, and equally shared the dangers of the Plains. No more women than men went mad in the isolation. When abandoned or widowed, they often went on to prosperity and wealth. Often they were the driving force behind their husbands coming to this dangerous country in the first place.

Many women saw the chance to homestead as one of the few ways for them to support themselves and even prosper. Many had no inclination toward marriage or remarriage but rather were determined to go it on their own. In fact, for many years, divorce was much more liberal on the Plains, and certain territories and states were viewed as havens for divorce-seekers because of their short residence requirements for divorces. Divorces were permitted in cases of impotency, adultery, prolonged absence (usually two years), extreme or repeated cruelty, and even intemperance. When women found themselves on their own, they often turned to traditionally male jobs to survive. Although there were prostitutes scattered throughout the Plains, most women became settlers, teamsters, laborers, seamstresses, laundresses, teachers, nurses, or whatever else it took to survive rather than submit to the degradation of life as a "sporting lady" or "soiled dove." Any role that a modern-day woman might choose for her living history persona would probably be accurate. It is true that the majority of women were married, but it is also public record that as many as twenty percent of homestead claims made were filed by women on their own.

Family Responsibilities

One of the burdens that women did bear on the Plains was that of giving birth to children. The production of children was one of the most important economic functions of women. This role bore heavily upon their health and often left them

Expensive Dress—This post-Civil War image can be a perfect source for a lady's reenactment outfit. The large check pattern is typical of an expensive dress and is somewhat economically biased. The cut of the sleeves and shape of the skirt are also representative of the Civil War era.

physically deformed and crippled. Gynecology was almost unknown to medical practice and often left them racked with female ailments, weaknesses, diseases, and other problems. Because of standards of modesty, women used a small female doll to show where the problem was. Treatment often included cauterization of the womb with a hot poker or a clitoridectomy. Little wonder that the company of another woman, no matter what her race, creed, or color, was of such great importance to women. Because of this, it was often the case that on many isolated ranches, trading posts, or farms young women were often enlisted as help when they were available.

As far as household duties were concerned, women were expected to cook, clean, sew, haul water, preserve food, make candles and soap, help with the farming, watch the children, and provide for much of their education. A matriarchal hierarchy often developed on the Plains, especially if the husband's work demanded that he be gone for long periods of time. Most women could shoot or handle livestock as well as most men of the time and sometimes even better. Long separations from spouses were often the case, especially concerning military marriages. It wasn't unusual at all for women to return back east when their children came to an age when they needed formal education, as many frontier military outposts had no facilities for schools. During the Civil War, many women found themselves on their own for several years while their husbands, brothers, and fathers were engaged in military service.

Because of the great demands placed on these home fronts, children were put to work at an early age. Toddlers and infants accompanied their mothers into the fields and were a constant source of concern. Very young children were given responsibilities that today might almost be considered abusive. It would not have been unusual at all to expect a five- or six-year-old to put in a full day's work of chores. Indoor and farmstead chores fell to the girls, while outdoor labor and herding were the boys' jobs. But when boys weren't available, girls would do fine. More than a few mothers were concerned with the fact that their daughters looked, worked, and acted like men. It was also because of these conditions that it would not be unreasonable to expect a twelve- or fourteen-year-old to assume the responsibilities of an adult it if conditions called for it.

As far as the lot of the American Indian woman of the Plains is concerned, her conditions were even worse. She labored under conditions of near slave-like servitude in some societies. However, in other cultures and tribes, she was allowed the same or even more opportunities than white women. She often held a great deal of leverage within her own household but was seldom allowed the role of leadership. The questions of survival for her family and herself must have been grim indeed at times.

Review of Women's Dress

The dress of the frontier woman varied according to the work that she was called upon to do. The dress was the universal outfit for the woman. Standards of the time dictated that women not wear pants in spite of their popularity today. Most women tried to keep their dresses simple for work and in remote areas, so a form of rather shapeless, sack-like garment was used. It was important to maintain feminine appearance, so even these dresses were often tied in the middle to preserve female curves. Like men's clothing, the styles often stayed the same no matter what the social standing was. And it was the material used, rather than the style, that dictated the value of the garment. Women wore their clothes in layers, and underwear as we know it today did not exist. Bras and panties didn't have much function back then. Bindings for the breasts and long skirts served instead.

Shoes were whatever could be had, and ladies' leather shoes were often small versions of men's work boots. Being "barefoot and pregnant" was not a joke on the Plains in the 19th century but rather a condition of life for many frontier women.

Sewing machines did not come along until the 1850s, so the spinning wheel and loom were very much a part of household equipment. This hand spinning and sewing

Carriage Coat—This type of coat was often worn during cold weather indoors since many frontier buildings were drafty and uncomfortable. This coat is economically biased.

naturally kept the number of buttons and ornamentation limited. The best advice is to keep all living history outfits simple. The more ornamentation there is, the more difficult it is to document the outfits. This is especially true of lace and beadwork. That is also why the common shawl is the easiest and most accurate method of reproducing light jackets or coats. It was popular with all women and in the form of the poncho was good for men's clothing as well.

Women of the time kept their heads covered, especially when outdoors. The simple bonnet was very popular, but like men, almost anything would do in a pinch. An old felt hat or head scarf was better than nothing. This applies to reenactors as well.

Women used, abused, and believed in the apron. With so many different jobs to do, an apron for wiping the hands and protecting valuable dresses was an absolute must. There was enough washing, ironing, and sewing to do without the invaluable services that an apron provided in saving wear on a valuable dress.

Many women of the Plains owned only two dresses. One was for wearing and the other for the wash. A special dress for special occasions was a true luxury and tended to be as fancy as the household could afford. During times of pregnancy, the sash or tie around the middle became looser, but the same dress still served its purpose. Today we tend to think in terms of halves when we design clothing, the waist being somewhere near the navel. Before the 1870s, styles of clothing were divided into thirds, with the waist of a garment for both men and women being at the base of the rib cage. This accounts for the high-waisted pants and skirts. This is also why camisole tops were long enough at the time but seem short to women of today.

For black powder reenactment to continue to grow today, it is very important that women and children be included in the activities. Women can gain a great

deal of insight into the thinking habits and philosophy of their female ancestors by examining their past through living history encounters. It is an insight that can give women and men a new appreciation for what has developed today in our society. It also allows a vivid look into the hard, gritty, exhaustive role of the women of the past, as well as a new perspective of the independent growth of women today. Questions of women's rights concerns, and demands for equal opportunity can be more fully examined and understood by all.

Girl's Outfit—A good example of early 19th century dress with mob cap and apron.

7

Portraying Women of
the Plains

IN ORDER TO RE-CREATE THE DRESS AND APPEARANCE OF
women of any time period, a thorough examination of the character is the first and
foremost obligation that must be undertaken. This will require a certain mindset
that you may not have attempted before. To be truly successful, the reenactor needs
to do more than just adopt different clothing. The inner being must be examined
and adopted as well. You must adopt your character's persona and step into that
character's role. Those questions of who you are, what you are, when you lived,
where you lived, and why you are in a certain location or situation must be thoroughly thought out. Reading and study will be the first step that must be undertaken to answer these five elements of character development.

Accurate Reenactment Considerations

Among the many aspects that you will need to consider are religion, age, social
and economic standing, marital and domestic standing, and familiarity with your
surroundings. You will need to write out a character profile of your persona and
create as full and as complex an individual as any person alive today. Perhaps a good
way to begin in this study is to ask yourself the question, "If I was there, how would
I be different than I am now?" This is a far more complex question than it would
seem at first thought. Chances are very likely that you would be totally different
in almost every aspect of your being and philosophy. We are all the products of
our environment and, as you read in the last chapter, the environments available to
women of 150 years ago were drastically different than those of today. You must be
open-minded and be willing to consider all possibilities.

It is vital that you consider the norm in your investigations. More advanced interpreters may want to attempt a more bizarre situation or character, but it is really better that the beginner settle for the average person to do a credible reenactment.

Pre-1800 Sketch—An effective and inexpensive outfit for rendezvous and reenactment. This figure exhibits a simple chemise undershirt (one sleeve shown full and the other short and gathered with a ribbon tie), a square pattern skirt with drawstring tie, and front draw camisole. The hat is low-crowned, broad-brimmed straw with fabric ties. A mob cap is usually worn under the straw hat. The camisole is of muslin or 100% cotton. The skirt may be of cotton, or if weather is cold, a heavier material such as wool may be used.

Early 1800s Sketch—Exhibiting characteristics of the early 1800s, this high-waist dress is complimented by the ever-present apron and shawl of muslin. The sleeves should be a bit tighter fit than is depicted. The morning cap or mob cap (also of muslin or some plain material) finishes an outfit that is accurate through the 1800-1840 period.

1830-40 Pioneer Woman—A simple work shirt of the same essential pattern worn by men, belted or tied at the waist, and worn outside the skirt is a good example of frontier women's work wear. Mated with an apron

and a full-length, drawstring skirt, this combination provides an excellent and functional outfit. The bonnet is a slated stiff brim style sewn to the fabric gather with full shoulder protection that is designed to fully frame the face and protect the neck and shoulders. This bonnet was worn on the Plains for decades. Be sure to allow a method of removing the cardboard slats in the brim before laundering.

Hispanic Outfit—This is the popular Southwest outfit of most of the early to late 19th century. Mexican women were common on the Plains as far north as Taos and were not unusual on the Santa Fe Trail. This outfit features the rebozo for headgear. The neck line is low and wide. Her bodice is not fitted and is of the chemise type except that the shirttail is often worn inside the skirt. The skirt should have a natural waist, be of dark colors, and have a full bell shape. Her shoes greatly resemble soft toe dancing slippers or she may wear moccasins.

Historic accuracy requires consideration of three factors. Every article of clothing, any artifact, and all activities must pass the "have," "want," and "afford" investigation process. Could your character have had it, would your character have wanted it, and should that person have been able to afford it?

Mexican Girl Outfit—This young lady is decked out in an easy and inexpensive style of dress.

Practical Girl's Outfit—Our tow-headed Indian presents something of a paradox. Still, this ribbon dress is a good outfit for a young lady at a rendezvous.

The technological question of accuracy is what the "have" question is concerned with. Obviously zippers, plastics, fake suede, nylon hosiery, and support bras fall completely from consideration. Little questions of buttons versus hooks, styles of patterns, and exact tools available become the central theme of your study.

The "want" consideration deals with cultural norms of the period and location. Even though makeup existed for hundreds of years before your character, that does not mean that she would have worn it. What is considered attractive today may have been considered outrageous and unacceptable then. Standards of modesty have fluctuated throughout history and you must make yourself aware of and be willing to accept the dictums of time and location. Don't go by motion pictures that are designed to appeal to modern audiences. You must put yourself in the position of pleasing people of your character's time. Read your journals carefully and critically evaluate what is being said and how it is being presented.

The "afford" concern speaks to the issue of economic accuracy. This can get complex because there is a great deal of economic bias in many pictures of the period.

Remember that having your picture taken back then was a rare and expensive undertaking. Naturally you would dress in your very best for this once-in-a-lifetime experience. Remember how you dressed for your prom picture? How accurate would it be to re-create everyday life in your high school years by dressing in your prom dress and attending class? The same principle applies in reenactment. Women didn't pass down their everyday work clothes. Only the very finest clothing would be saved and even at that, only wealthier women would be able to do so.

Everyday clothing was worn until it was rags and then literally used as rags until it had no future value. Again, it is important to remember that while labor is far more expensive than materials today, in the early 19th century, the reverse was true.

Every effort was made to construct garments so that they would last. Skirts were designed so that they could be "turned" as many as four times. Since long skirts would naturally fray and wear at the bottom, dresses were designed so that when the fraying became too noticeable, the skirt would be reversed and resewn at the the top. When the process of fading and fraying became too advanced, the skirt would be resewn inside-out and the process would begin again.

Because material was so expensive, solid-colored fabrics or geometric patterns that could not be considered right side up or upside down, and which could be easily turned and patched, were the most popular. Large patterns were reserved for only expensive dresses because it was so difficult to match large patterns without a great deal of waste. Small patterns were much more practical and popular. Many garments were "pieced." Bits of fabric were sewn together with the patterns matched,

Pre-Civil War Ladies—Linda Luzader and Angel Headlee in functional dresses of the pre-Civil War period. Note Angel's 1840s style slippers and Linda's morning cap.

then used as if they were a single piece of fabric. Because upper body perspiration would naturally be a problem and quite likely stain and ruin valuable material, most dresses were double lined with a cheaper material to protect the outside appearance of a dress. Including this lining for the collar, underarms, and breasts is essential for accurate reenactment.

Growing girls often had built-in growth tucks incorporated into their dresses. A one- or two-inch tuck sewn into a skirt gave the garment extended life. These women were so expert at sewing that these tucks in the skirt or at the sides of the bodice are barely noticeable. Again, a further case for solid or small pattern dresses for young women becomes mandatory. Drawstrings at the waist and along the top of the bodice gave the garment flexibility as young girls grew and developed. Shoes and boots are an expensive item of clothing for the newcomer. Cheap China slippers are a reasonable solution but be aware of round toes and rubber soles that are not historically accurate. Thrift shops often contain extremely square-toed pumps from the 1960s but it may be necessary to have the heels cut down to no higher than one inch. If early felt spats are attached over the pumps, convincing cloth-top boots of the period can be created. Round-toed slippers are accurate for Hispanic dress of the period and can be easily documented.

In the 1840s, India rubber boots were very popular among women and often mentioned in journals for use in sloppy weather. Moccasins are usually a good alternative for everyday work shoes for plains women. Expensive Amish boots are a good solution if you want to spend the money. Just make sure that they have a square, flat toe and a leather upper.

While fashion did influence headwear, practicality was also an important consideration. Women were generally consistent in their adherence to fashion. A woman dressed in plain, unfashionable clothing of the rural homesteader would not wear a fancy, decorated hat. It would have been simple like the dress. For women of the Plains, a standard slatted work bonnet would be the most appropriate. It would be constructed with an economic use of fabric, even piecing of leftovers, and be without ribbon ties or lace work. Be sure that the slats can be removed and replaced as needed.

Straw hats were popular after 1849 for average dress but were seldom worn with formal dresses. It would be about as appropriate as a modern-day man wearing a three-piece suit with a baseball cap. A fancy dress would dictate a fancy bonnet, but you must answer the question of likelihood of a fancy outfit being worn on the early Plains. The simpler your reenactment outfit, the better.

Style Suggestions

If you choose the popular Spanish outfit of the Southwest, you must include a rebozo for headwear. A rebozo was a cloth scarf that wrapped about the head and hung down over the shoulders. It also functioned as a shawl in the evenings. Going without a rebozo is inaccurate and hurts your credibility. Examine paintings and photos of women of the Spanish culture of the 1820s to 1860s. The rebozo head covering is always present in all but the most formal outfits.

The universal hairstyle of almost all women of this time period was the center parted, pulled back style. What you do with the rest of your hair depends on the time periods and race of your reenactment.

Using a rebozo or head scarf is a good way to disguise the modern short hairstyles of today's women. You can center part your short hair and hold it with mousse or hairspray and look quite authentic. Remember that the part of your body which people notice first is your face. It is negligent to concentrate on the accuracy of dress and not consider the face and hair.

If you choose to portray an Indian woman, it is absolutely essential that you do not mix tribal traditions and variations inappropriately. Indian women seldom wore a head covering, but they did not bare their legs. Botas should reach above the skirt line on Indian women's outfits.

If you are choosing to portray a woman of the late 1820s and 1830s, you

Mexican Outfit—Joy Klein in a Mexican laborer's dress. She is wearing common babriccos mocs and a leather possibles bag. A Mexican woman of this period and of Joy's age would also be wearing a rebozo head covering.

Native American Outfit—P. J. Harrington in an accurate Cheyenne woman's outfit. The jewelry and neckband would have been reserved for special occasions such as a visit to the fort.

need to concentrate on a wide, modest neckline on your dress with diagonal lines in the bodice and curved side seams on the bodice back. Your dress should fasten in the back and have full upper arm sleeves and a short sleeve length. The armscye should be diagonal and tight. The skirt should be wide and the shape should be full and of ankle length. Morning caps were very popular and your shoes should be generally slipper-like with square, flat toes and low or nonheeled.

In the 1840s women turned from the morning cap to the bonnet. Dresses should have a "jewel" neckline which is round at the nape of the neck. The bodice and bodice back should be fan shaped to increase the look of width at the shoulders. The dress should fasten in the back and have tight-fitting sleeves that reach to the mid-forearm. The waist should be at or just below the natural waist with an exaggerated point. The skirt should be full and worn with multiple petticoats. Your shoes would be much the same as the earlier period but you may wear pumps or boots.

A woman of the 1850s may wear a hat, as hats found new favor in the styles of that era. Bonnets should outline and frame the face. The bodice of the dress should be gathered with curved side seams but should not accentuate the bosom. It should button in the front.

The sleeves are full, especially in the forearm, and should be wrist length. The waist is

Anglo Woman's Dress—Jaunita Leisch in standard Anglican dress of the 1840s. Her rebozo headgear was much favored by all women in marginal weather. Juanita believes that the bodice should be tighter in the waist for accuracy.

Woman's Boot—A close-up of Jaunita's woman's boot of the 1840s. Elastic side gussets on the boot are accurate for the 1850s.

natural and the waist seam straight. The skirt width is exaggerated and maintained with the use of hoops. The skirt length would be toe top or floor length, but remember that prairie women would not allow their skirt bottoms to drag in the dirt. They would seldom use hoops for working dresses. The heels of the shoes may now go up to one inch. The general look is to try to appear broad and short. Images of Mary Todd Lincoln are good examples.

Common materials for all outfits should be of a type that was available at the time. Cottons, serge, flannel, wools, and satin are all acceptable and historically accurate.

A traditional Mexican woman would have a rebozo head covering. Her neckline would be wide and low. Her bodice would not be fitted and would be more of a chemise type, except that the shirttail would be worn inside the skirt. Her sleeves would be cut straight and often short. The skirt would have a waist at natural height and the waist seam would be straight. Her skirt would be fully bell-shaped and only of mid-calf length. She would wear low-cut shoes or moccasins. She would favor a light-colored top and a red or dark blue skirt. A center part in her hair would tell that she is married, while a side part would indicate an unmarried status. She would be more likely to braid her hair and allow the braids to hang to her shoulders. As an older woman, she would favor dark colors for formal dress, especially if she is of the upper class.

I am certainly not going to attempt to tell women how to sew. Lord knows that my first feeble attempts were not very impressive. One point should be made, however. If reenactment is a goal, then those seams that show should be hand sewn. It is a trifling point, but it does aid in authenticity.

Resources for Women's Study

Juanita Leisch, whose shoe lectures were of great value to me in writing this chapter, suggests the following bibliography of books that might be useful in researching women's dress:

Down the Santa Fe Trail and into Mexico: The Diary of Susan Shelby Magoffin, 1846–1847. Edited by Stella M. Drumm. University of Nebraska Press, Lincoln, 1962.

Root of Bitterness: Documents of Social History of American Women. Edited by Nancy Cott. Northeastern University Press, Boston, 1986

Pioneer Women: Voices from the Kansas Frontier. Joanna L. Stratton. Simon & Schuster, New York, 1981.

Eyewitness to War: Prints and Daguerreotypes of the Mexican War, 1846–1848. Martha Sandweiss et al. Published by Amon Carter Museum, Fort Worth, TX. Available from the Smithsonian Institution Press, Washington, DC.

Costume in Detail: Women's Dress 1730–1930. Nancy Bradfield. Plays Inc., Boston, 1968. (Constructional notes are unsurpassed anywhere. Beware: information is economically biased and European.)

The History of Underclothes. C. Willett & Phillis Cunnington. Faber and Faber, Boston, 1981. (Photographs and descriptions of original garments. Beware: information is economically biased and European.)

The Family Album: Ladies Wear Daily. Juanita Leisch. Wearlooms, Berryville, VA, 1988. (Includes fifty photographs taken of women of the Civil War period but they are in their best dress, which increases economic bias.)

I would also like to include some recommendations that I have found very valuable on this subject:

The Female Frontier, A Comparative View of Women on the Prairie and the Plains. Glenda Riley. University Press of Kansas, Lawrence, KS, 1988. (A very good, if somewhat scholarly, account of women in the middle and late 19th century. Excellent for gaining insight into the early plains woman.)

On the Santa Fe Trail. Edited by Marc Simmons. University Press of Kansas, Lawrence, KS, 1986. (A collection of original accounts of travel on the Santa Fe Trail. Several references are made about women as well as writings by women. It is very enlightening.)

The Book of Buckskinning I-V. Edited by William H. Scurlock. Rebel Publishing Company, Texarkana, TX, 1981–1988. (You will probably want to examine the contents of these books before making your selections, unless you want the whole series. Book IV is valuable for early clothing patterns.)

Women of the West. Cathy Luchetti, in collaboration with Carol Olwell. Antelope Island Press, St. George, UT, 1982. (This book is a collection of diaries of several women in various representative time periods. It provides easy access for beginner's to obscure sources. There are many interesting photographs and a very fine diary by Mary Richardson Walker for pre-1840s observations.)

The Workwoman's Guide. Opus Publications, Guilford, CT, 1986. (This is a reprint of an original 1838 sewing and pattern book written by a wealthy lady who preferred to remain unknown yet wanted to provide instructions as part of charity work. It is difficult to locate but can be ordered from James D. Hayden, Book

Peddler, 88360 Charly Lane, Springfield, OR 97478, (503) 746-1819. It is fascinating reading.

Authentic patterns for 19th century women's clothing may be ordered from:

Lorraine Micke
88360 Charly Lane
Springfield, OR 97478
(503) 746-1819

Boys' Outfits—These young gentlemen are demonstrating acceptable outfits for boys. Notice the cut of the shorts and drop-front pants. The boy on the left is wearing common moccasins and the lad on the right is in square toe boots of the period.

8

Rendezvous

ANYONE WHO GETS VERY INVOLVED IN BLACK POWDER ACTIVI-
ties is going to run into the rendezvous. The term originally applied to a type of wild
and woolly "trading convention" that was held for mountain men in the wilds of the
Rockies from 1824 to 1840. Trappers would bring in their furs to barter for goods

Traders' Row Activities—The crowded festival atmosphere of Traders' Row at
rendezvous is only part of the fun. Many unusual crafts may be purchased.

and supplies to get them through the coming season. Needless to say, these affairs could get pretty hairy and certainly involved drunkenness, whoring, gambling, fighting, and any other activity that lonely, independent, and violent men might engage in after a year or so of isolation. It was certainly not a place for the faint of heart or the ultraconservative.

Today, rendezvous has a totally different connotation. The term "encampment" would probably be a more fitting term for the activities that take place, but the romantic ideal of the rendezvous keeps the term alive, even if it really doesn't describe the event. To state it simply, a rendezvous is a gathering of black powder enthusiasts for the purpose of fun! All activities are centered around a pre-1840 or primitive spirit. It involves shooting contests, socializing, knife and tomahawk throwing contests, camping (both modern and primitive), trading, primitive skills contests, and many other activities too numerous to mention. It is, in essence, a costume party, usually set around the pre-1840 time period, that is specifically oriented for black powder interests. But do not be deviced. Many a "rondy-vooer" could care less about shooting a black powder weapon. It has become a social event first and foremost, and in recent years it has become more and more a family function. This trend seems very likely to continue in the future. The days of male-only mountain-man-type gatherings are long gone. For a rendezvous to succeed today, it needs to appeal to women and children as well as to a bunch of old bachelor buckskinners. For some this has ruined the idea of the rendezvous, but for the vast majority, the idea of an event that involves and entertains the entire family, from the youngsters right up to grandpa and grandma, has made this the fastest-growing aspect of black powder interests.

Spirit versus Authenticity

It is the goal of most rendezvous activities to preserve the visible spirit of a pre-1840 encampment. It is impossible for most people to re-create exactly a primitive encampment of the time period because the expense would be prohibitive. That is why the term "spirit" is such an important consideration. What this means is the ideal is approximated

Rendezvous Twins—Such rendezvous sights as these boys in matching outfits are part of the entertainment and help provide many rendezvous memories.

Campfire Friends—Socializing around the campfire is a big part of modern rendezvous.

as closely as is practical. Buffalo hide tipis would cost as much as a small house and therefore are replaced for rendezvous with considerably less expensive canvas copies. Canvas tents were not all that prevalent, but people must be sheltered and there is really little alternative. Tin ware and wooden dishes are authentic but very difficult to find, so enamelware is often substituted. But the line is drawn when someone decides to use Tupperware or plastic or paper plates. That ruins the "spirit," even though the enamelware is not truly authentic. Most camp cooking is done over an open fire on cast-iron cookware, even though the old-timers probably didn't have much cast iron to lug over the mountains. Camp chairs of rough wood are fine because most people like the comfort, even though most of those old mountain men just didn't pack them. However, a modern lawn chair is totally unacceptable because that ruins the primitive atmosphere. Therefore, unlike a reenactment, where everything is as accurate as it can possibly be, a rendezvous allow more items that are in the spirit of primitive ideals and materials, even if not 100% accurate. There are sometimes heated debates among participants concerning where that line between authenticity and spirit should be drawn, but that is inevitable in this type of activity.

Terminology

To best describe a rendezvous, it is helpful to first give a typical list of rules and terms that apply to most of these gatherings. The rules are usually very simple, and each gathering is greatly influenced by the "booshway" of the event. The booshway is the official man or woman in charge. He or she is usually supported by a co-booshway or *segundo*, a scribe (bookkeeper), a shooting range officer, a trade committee, and, if the event has them present, a corral manager for livestock. Rules are enforced by "dog soldiers" who are a type of police force for the event. A "flatlander" or "pilgrim" is what you are until you get the feel of things and have some idea of what you are doing. How do you tell the difference? When you get there, you'll know.

Typical Rendezvous Rules

*   Rendezvous usually run three to four days with larger nationals often encompassing a nine- to eleven-day gathering. A set of representative rules are as follows:
*   The "dog soldiers" are the booshway's representatives. Please refer disagreements to the booshway. (His or her word is law in camp.)
*   Primitive camp will close to vehicles after 10:00 PM.

Dixie Squirrel Rifle—A perfect percussion sidelock for the rendezvous is this full stock .32 caliber Dixie Squirrel rifle.

Keep vehicles on main roads as much as possible. Look for your site on foot, then drive to it only to unload. (There is usually a one- or two-hour limit on unloading and loading camp materials.)

Vehicles are allowed in primitive camp only to unload and load up camps.

Persons reentering primitive camp with a vehicle without specific permission will load up camp and depart!

Park your vehicle in the parking area after you unload in primitive camp but before you set up camp.

Handicapped or impaired persons may get permission for special parking through permission of the booshway.

Controlled pets are welcome but all pets shall be leashed at all times. (The trend toward no pets allowed is steadily growing and will certainly continue in the future.)

Owners of barking and free-running pets will be warned only once and then asked to leave.

Lost parents can be found at the flagpole (the usual meeting place at most rendezvous).

Sharpshooter—As rendezvous interests changed, black powder cartridge shooting contests were allowed at many gatherings.

Open fires are permitted if favorable conditions exist. Attend all fires and report all unattended fires that you find. You must have a fire bucket and shovel in your camp. No cigarette butts are to be put on the ground. They must be put in the fire ring.

Do not cut or damage live trees. (Fire wood is usually provided. It is usually good insurance to bring some of your own.)

Clean up your camp when you leave and have a dog soldier check you out of camp. (There is often a camp deposit that will be refunded when you leave and pass inspection.)

No modern firearms in camp. No unauthorized cannons may be fired in camp.

No cap-and-ball revolvers are worn in camp. (Sometimes, however, they are allowed for shooting events.)

Load weapons only at the range or during special events.

Only primitive dress may be worn after 6:00 PM in the primitive area. No trading in the modern camp. All goods must be displayed in a primitive manner. (Modern packaging is usually not allowed.)

No rowdy behavior will be tolerated after 11:00 PM

Acceptable Dress

Perhaps the most common question asked by someone who is considering taking part in a rendezvous is what is meant by primitive dress. Generally it can be said that it is relatively simple for most people to come up with a basic outfit. A simple cotton shirt of old style, a pair of pants (avoid blue jeans), and a pair of moccasins or brogans (square-toed work shoes), or even Wellington boots, is enough to get a first timer by. A simple shapeless ribbon dress or shirt and skirt will work for women and girls. Boys and men often will start out with a pair of corduroy pants with the back pockets and belt loops removed. The rest of the sins can be covered by the long tails of a shirt. A calico shirt that is more than adequate can usually be purchased from traders for less than $30. Women often begin their outfits with a shirt over a skirt.

Avoid the use of ball caps, polyesters, zippers (unless hidden), tennis shoes (nothing fouls up an outfit quicker than a pair of Nikes), blue jeans, modern jewelry, plastics, cowboy hats, modern cowboy boots, and metal snaps on shirts. The use of a radio or cassette player is usually very unappreciated. Avoid them at all costs. You will learn the rest as you become more involved in the hobby. Rondy-vooers are a forgiving lot if a person makes an honest effort.

Modern campers (tin tipis) and nylon tents are placed in a separate area, out of view of the primitive camp, so those who are more advanced can enjoy their primitive experience. But there is certainly no disgrace for those who have not been able to make the investment in primitive gear. As long as you are in primitive dress, the primitive camp can be visited after the curfew, and those gatherings around the campfire after dark are often among the greatest pleasures. For those of you with small children, a modern camper may be your only alternative for a while. No one should miss out on the pleasures of the rendezvous just because of the inability to attend in a 100% primitive fashion at first. One of the advantages of modern rendezvous is that it is a very inexpensive vacation, with camp fees rarely running over $50.

Advantages and Disadvantages

There are a few disadvantages to rendezvous. It is often difficult to have a ready supply of fresh water on hand because of the locations. Get in the habit of bringing plenty for your use. This is a primitive experience so plan on close encounters with insects, critters, unpleasant plants, less-than-appealing reptiles, and an abundant supply of dirt. A first aid kit and insect repellent, especially if there are youngsters, are absolutely essential. Outdoor johns are always provided but an extra supply of toilet paper is a wise investment.

Unless you have refrigeration in a camper, plan to take foods that are easy to keep and prepare. This is no place for frozen chicken and meats, potato salad, and chocolate candy bars. Canned goods and dried foods are much more practical. Ice is often provided by the rendezvous management but its availability shouldn't be taken for granted. Plan accordingly. There are often food vendors at rendezvous but a good supply of fill-ins always makes good sense.

On the plus side is the presence of a number of friendly folks and enjoyable people. The arts and crafts present are numerous and often quite well executed. It's amazing what kinds of trinkets, doodads, tools, and skills one will encounter.

There are usually planned events for children, and some rendezvous have classes to help the newcomers and experienced alike learn more about primitive lifestyles.

A large sampling of folk music and old-time musical instruments, something that is generally a surprise for the newcomer, is always present, especially around the evening campfires. Since the activity is centered on black powder there are numerous shooting events and a great deal of practical knowledge to be gained from the activity.

General Suggestions for Rendezvous

Practical advice concerning the rendezvous is often worth considering. Go slowly in deciding on an outfit and persona. Learn from experienced rendezvous participants before investing in clothing or materials that you may not be satisfied with in the long run. Be particular about that you purchase from traders. Get the real thing and do not be satisfied with counterfeit or low-quality merchandise. Attend several gatherings before making any large purchases or commitments. Pat-

Stepping Back in Time—Hunting in a rendezvous outfit is a popular extension of the rendezvous spirit.

terns of period clothing can be purchased from traders and a great deal of money can be saved by making much of your clothing and other materials yourself.

Don't be discouraged by one poorly planned rendezvous. A rendezvous is only as good as the booshway and, unfortunately, some of them are not good planners. When you go to a good one, you'll know it. The superior organization is always obvious. Go during different times of the year. Summer rendezvous, except in the high mountains, can often be endurance contests in the heat. Try some of the spring and fall gatherings on weekends. These are often the most enjoyable, certainly where the weather is concerned. Join an organization if you become interested. There are numerous state and local clubs where you can get schedules and make new acquaintances. Membership in the National Muzzle Loading Rifle Association (NMLRA) is extremely important.

The most important element to the rendezvous is you. This is an activity that can be loads of fun or just another hectic headache. A lot of what it is depends on the attitudes that you carry with you. If you are tolerant and willing to let others learn as you have had to; if you are one who enjoys the outdoors and outdoor activities; if you are a person who enjoys old-time crafts, music, and humor; if you are just a little bit eccentric and enjoy yourself and others for that quality; if you have thick skin and a good sense of humor, then rondyvooing is probably for you.

No, it isn't for everyone. But then neither is black powder, living history, or reenactment. On the other hand, the activity can be a very pleasurable experience if you are so inclined. For some of us it beats the heck out of sitting at home watching the boob tube, and it is certainly a more productive activity.

9

Black Powder Accessories

IF YOU HAVEN'T PURCHASED YOUR FIRST BLACK POWDER RIFLE or pistol yet but are saving up the bucks to do so, you had better plan on spending at least $60 more. I hate to burst your bubble but there are certain items that you are going to need that are not usually included with the weapon. You will probably spend more than the $60 in the long run but it will take that much to begin shooting.

Black Powder and Pyrodex

Of course you can't shoot a black powder weapon without powder. No matter what you may have heard, no matter what excuses you might be able to come up with, you must use only black powder or Pyrodex in your weapon. Smokeless powder will never work under any conditions unless you have some kind of death wish. For most shooters, there are three grades of black powder that should be used.

FFFFg is an extremely fine grained powder that produces high pressures and is used for priming flintlocks. FFFg black powder is used for weapons up to .50 caliber. Pistols should be shot with this grade of powder unless they are larger than .50 caliber. FFg powder is used in weapons larger than .50 caliber. The only brand of black powder that I know of that is commonly marketed on the plains today is Goex, Inc. Superfine Black Rifle Powder. If you don't see it on your local sporting goods store shelf, ask for it. It is usually kept under lock and key, separate from the smokeless powder, because of federal regulations.

Shooting Bag—
Essentials for a percussion gun shooting bag are nipple wrench, vent pick, short starter, powder measure, capper, ball bag, and powder horn.

Black powder does have some drawbacks that are inherent to the beast. It is somewhat unstable and fouls weapons quickly. I can usually get only three shots out of my .54 cal. before I need to run a cleaning patch down the barrel. To try to get around these drawbacks, Hodgdon Powder Company of Shawnee Mission, Kansas, markets a substitute propellant under the brand name of Pyrodex. Pyrodex will produce more shots per pound, a cleaner burn which alleviates fouling, and very constant pressures and velocities. It is also easier to find in many areas because of shipping regulations. It is currently available in three grades: RS for rifle and shotgun, P for pistols, and CTG for cartridges and shotshells. Some companies will not warrant their products if Pyrodex is used in them. You need to check the warranty on the products if you are concerned. Both black powder and Pyrodex need to be stored in a cool, dry environment. I like to store both in a separate environment from the rest of my shooting supplies and away from snoops and children. It is also a wise decision to not mix carrying containers for Pyrodex and black powder if you use both. Label your containers to prevent confusion.

Doctor Gary White made two of the author's favorite muzzle-loaders. The rifle in the background is a .58-caliber plains rifle. The rifle in the foreground is a 12-bore English sporting rifle. With the right projectiles, either one is an excellent big-game rifle.

Patched Balls and Conicals

Your next decision will be the type of projectile to shoot. You have the choice of patched round ball or a bullet. Bullets, also referred to as conicals, have the advantages of weight and stability. I am of the opinion that patched round balls are a bit more accurate. Bullets enjoy quite a bit of advantage. However, for light-boned game such as deer, I have never felt the need for the conical's heavier hitting power. When hunting elk or bear, I do believe there is a tremendous advantage in using conicals.

There are some things that you need to know about your weapon before you purchase it if you have a preference for either round balls or conicals. The first is the weapon's depth of rifling. Conicals work best in a barrel with shallow groves of .004" to .005". Round balls are more efficient with grooves of .010" to .012".

The second is the weapon's rate of twist of the rifling. Twists of 1-66" are more efficient for round balls, while conicals perform better with a twist of 1-48". There are other twist rates available but these are the most common. If you choose a patched round ball, I suggest that you buy precut patches to begin with until you are totally familiar with the weapon. I prefer Ox-Yoke pre-lubed patches, but there

Shotgun Accessories—The author's shotgun shooting bag includes a shot snake with charger measure, powder and shot measure, powder flask, capper, and short starter to start tight wads.

are several brands of patches on the market. There is also a large selection of patch lubes available. I don't recommend using spit to lube a patch as it dries out too soon to suit me. I have found that old smokeless tobacco containers are excellent for storing extra patches. They help keep pre-lubed patches from drying out and they help keep all patches clean.

Necessary Accessories

I suggest that a beginner consider buying some sort of shooter's kit when purchasing a new weapon. There are some excellent kits available, especially from CVA and Navy Arms. These kits usually contain a powder flask, lubricant, bullet seat, powder measure, some caps, and a capper. Some include a nipple wrench and lead balls as well. You are going to need all of these items, and purchasing a kit is a good way of not forgetting anything.

There are several brands of caps available. Most modern replicas use #11-size caps, but if you purchase a large single-shot pistol or a musket, they you will need to check on what size caps they will need. Pistols, especially revolvers, often use #10-size caps. Purchasing a capper, which is a device to hold and feed percussion caps, is an absolute must unless you make one out of a thin piece of leather. One trip afield will prove just how difficult it is to manage these caps with the fingers, especially if you suffer from the "fumbles" as I do.

A nipple wrench, which acts as a wrench for unscrewing percussion nipples from the rifle, is a tool that you will use whenever you clean your gun, and you really do need to clean it after every day's shooting. Most wrenches have nipple picks designed into them, and these are necessary as well. If you are going to hunt big game in adverse conditions, you might also consider a nipple primer. They do save much time and hassle and help make certain that your first, and maybe only, shot will ignite the powder charge.

Short starters, which are nothing more than short ramrods to ease the loading of balls and bullets, are safer for loading than trying it with a ramrod. Short starters can be easily made, but they really aren't expensive and last forever unless you lose one.

Because of the somewhat complex nature of muzzle-loading, I suggest that you carry some sort of trouble kit when you go afield with your gun. I carry mine in an old pipe tobacco pouch. It includes a screwdriver that fits the screws, a cleaning jag (a tool to hold cleaning patches), a ball puller, a small punch, a small wrench that fits #11 nipples, and an extra nipple. It has been called upon for service several times. Lyman markets a Sportsman's Keeper Kit that includes a brass hammer with brass drift pin, and excellent screwdriver, and a stubby ratchet screwdriver in a plastic storage box in high-visibility orange. It is perfect for the muzzleloader when combined with a good nipple wrench.

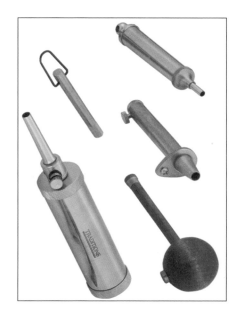

Accessories Kits—Kits such as this one from Traditions can be purchased as one unit to provide for the needs of most shooters. The kit includes a flintlock pan charger, powder measure, short starter, capper, and powder flask.

An extra ramrod is a good idea for longer hunting or shooting trips. Most ramrods are made of wood or fiberglass. Wood ramrods will break in the excitement of the moment. Mountain State Manufacturing markets the Super Rod. It is virtually indestructible but doesn't look very good for reenactment. There has been talk that a fiberglass ramrod will hurt the accuracy of a rifle over a period of years because of its abrasive qualities. If you choose to believe this, then you may want a muzzle guard to put on the ramrod to prevent any damage to the crown of the muzzle of your rifle. I like fiberglass ramrods and am of the opinion that it is poor cleaning techniques and inadequate care that are the real nemesis of the black powder weapon. A fiberglass ramrod is not nearly as damaging as a dirty wooden ramrod embedded with grime and sand. Common sense, folks, common sense.

Flasks, horns, and quickloaders are all available for carrying powder. Quickloaders are usually small plastic tubes that carry pre-measured amounts of powder as well as ball, bullet, or shot. They are handy, especially when hunting large game where you will probably get only a maximum of three or four shots per day. They are also quicker for loading follow-up shots. For longer outings where several shots will be taken, I prefer the flask or horn and a good loading block for patched round balls. A powder measure is necessary with either the flask or horn. It just isn't a good idea to pour powder directly into a weapon without using a measure. If something should go amiss, that's quite a little hand grenade you've got holding your powder. You could end up with the nickname of "Stubby." Don't think for a minute that the old-timers didn't use powder measures. They were usually made of horn or antler. Those old boys didn't have a death wish either. Most of you will end up carrying a knife with your muzzleloader. Those big Bowies are fine for reenactment and as a last-ditch defense against Injuns, but they are practically useless for anything else. I haven't heard of any Injun uprisings lately, so I usually leave mine at home. A much more practical knife is a small belt knife with a blade of about four inches, or a good-quality pocket knife. I have a Queens Steel knife that I have carried for close to thirty years. It's on its second handle and fourth scabbard. Buck and Schrade are also excellent knives that are commonly available. Don't get a cheap knife unless you intend to lose it.

Care and Cleaning Tips

Cleaning a muzzleloader is a relatively easy affair. Most shooters use hot, soapy water but there are several commercial solvents available. I like Birchwood Casey No. 77, especially when I'm going on overnight trips. Some other good brands are Spit-Bath from Hodgdon, Old Time from CVA, and Old Slickum, which can be ordered from Dixie Gun Works. The main thing to remember about cleaning is to not overdo the oiling at the end of the process and store a freshly cleaned gun with the muzzle down for drainage. If you run a dry patch down the muzzle before you

Shooting Bags—Sometimes called a possibles bag, these are two that the author carried. A leather purse was the first followed by a soft leather commercial bag. The author made the bag on the right, which includes a holstered patch knife and short starter.

begin your day's shooting and set off a couple of caps to clear the nipple, it will go a long way toward successful shooting and a minimum of misfires.

A 20 gauge bore brush used for cleaning shotguns works great for thoroughly cleaning the barrel of a .50 or .54 caliber, especially the buildup that occurs after several rounds of black powder shooting. There will be times that you may go on long hunting trips and not get back home until late. On those occasions it is not unusual to really not want to clean your muzzleloader that night. It has happened to me several times. If you place a small piece of leather over the nipple with the hammer down to prevent leakage, put a few ounces of solvent down the barrel, and allow it to set until you can clean the weapon the next day, you will not harm your gun and you'll probably be pleasantly surprised at how easily the gun will clean up.

Handguns

If you have a pistol, then you are going to need a holster. I made my reenactment holster using a grocery sack pattern and a single piece of leather. It looks and works great. For bad weather, I like to use a flapped holster to keep as much of the crud off my pistol as possible. Dixie markets several good holsters, as do a host of other companies. Uncle Mike's cordura holsters work very well if you are not a purist. After wielding those 7 ½" and 8" barreled .44's around for a while, I think you will realize why so many of the old–timers wore these big pistols in a cross-draw style. They didn't wear their pistols slung low like most movie gunfighters. They had work to do most of the time and the pistols were worn high to keep them out of the way. A cross draw is really a much more efficient way of drawing an 8" barreled revolver. Cross draw rigs also work better when sitting at a poker table or in a wagon box. Military men wore their pistols on the right cross draw fashion, because the right hand was for drawing sabers. The left hand was for drawing the pistol. Makes sense now, doesn't it?

Several firms market shoulder stocks for revolvers. One time out with one of these rigs will probably prove one too many. There are several reasons why cap and ball revolvers were fired at arm's length. The farther away you can shoot them from your face, the better.

Special Items

Shooting glasses are essential when shooting black powder. Pieces of percussion cap sometimes fly everywhere when they are fired. A piece of percussion cap in the eye is not a very attractive prospect to have to live with. Hearing protection in the form of plugs or muffs makes a great deal of sense when shooting several rounds . . .

Shooting glasses are essential when you are shooting a black-powder firearm.

that is, unless your are fond of saying "What?" every time someone speaks to you. Scopes are illegal in most states when hunting big game with muzzleloaders. They are quite handy for varmit shooting, however. Receiver sights aren't nearly as popular as they once were, but they really do significantly improve shooting and they are legal almost everywhere. Try them if you are not satisfied with your open sights. I believe that you will be pleasantly surprised.

A good book is always a handy item to have around when you have technical questions about your muzzle-loader. One of the very best is Lyman's *Black Powder Handbook*. It is full of load recommendations, trajectory tables, and general-interest articles. Another fine offering is Sam Fadala's *The Complete Black Powder Handbook*. I purchased this book with my first muzzle-loading rifle and have never regretted it. I have gone many times to both references when I've had questions. I've always found the answers in one or the other.

10

The Black Powder Trek

THE AUSTRALIANS CALL IT A WALKABOUT. TO MANY IT WOULD simply be called a camping and hunting trip. For myself, especially when carrying black powder weapons on the open plains, the two- or three-day black powder hunting and camping trip is best termed a trek. Since I have given up my horses because of the expense of upkeep, these long foot trips have become a major source of enjoyment. Whether it be over the brushy sandhills of south-central Kansas, the beautiful Flint Hills of the eastern third, or the broad open plains of the West, trekking not only becomes a good source of hunting, it has also provided some of the best wildlife encounters that I have ever experienced. There is something about these longer trips that goes especially well with blackpowder arms. The nostalgic feelings of wandering about in such a fashion truly give the participant the experience of past days of adventure. Luckily, there are several locations left throughout the plains where such experiences are possible. Large tracts of open pasture can be found, and if it is not during pheasant or deer seasons, permission for access is fairly easy to obtain. Throughout the West there are very large acreages of federal grasslands and forests where camping and hunting are legal and open to all. During the off-seasons, these huge areas are usually very lightly used and can provide some excellent opportunities for primitive experiences.

Supplies

The beauty of trekking is that it can be made as primitive or as modern as one wishes. With today's hiking and backpacking enthusiasm growing, lightweight, ultramodern synthetic supplies do, however, go against the grain when black pow-der arms are involved. On the other hand, when the weather turns cold, a modern sleeping bag sure has its advantages over wrapping up in wool blankets. I usually try to draw a happy medium unless organizational rules or special primitive trips are planned. It is difficult giving up those matches and Ziploc baggies if one doesn't have to.

The idea behind black powder trekking is to get the experience of roughing it and enjoying black powder hunting as well. This activity demands that the trekker takes the least amount of equipment possible. After just a few miles of hiking, one often wonders whether he brought too much. When camp is set, however, that same person often wishes that he had brought more. The trick, and much of the fun of the sport, is striking that happy medium.

I recently read a fellow's list of things that he took along on hunting and camp-ing trips. Either he doesn't go more than fifty yards from the truck or he must look like a traveling peddler as he drags his loot down the trails. To really enjoy the experience, it is imperative to travel light.

At the most, I want only a backpack, shooting bag and camera slowing me down or struggling with my rifle for attention. I certainly don't want the pack to weigh much more than twenty pounds. Adding a seven- to nine-pound black pow-der rifle, a backup pistol, and the shooting accessories that go along with them can get to be a pretty hefty load, especially in rough or dry country.

Period Correct Canteens—A canteen is vital for any reenactment when there is no easy source of water. These are made of gourds and leather.

Camp Life—Members of the "opposition," a Texas muzzle-loading and reenactment group, demonstrate a typical camp of the 1830s at Bent's Old Fort, Colorado.

Water

One of the major differences that will be noticed by experienced trekkers from other parts of the country when they venture onto the plains is the availability of water. Good clean water, which is easily available elsewhere, is difficult to come by, especially when making long treks on foot. The trekker needs to pack a lot of water with him. Water is heavy, but its importance is much greater than anything else that might be taken along. This is another reason why the pack needs to be as light as possible.

Clothing

Probably the best times of the year for trekking on the plains are the spring and fall. Unless there is a sudden storm, one can camp in comfort well into the month of November on the Southern Plains. Wearing clothing in layers is the best method of adjusting to sudden extremes that may arise during the day and night. A light cotton shirt worn under a heavier shirt gives a great deal of flexibility, especially if the trekker is also taking along a heavy coat. Not long ago, I purchased a medium-weight gray wool capote from Jim's Gun Shop in Sheridan, Missouri, that fits the bill perfectly for this type of activity. Worn over the two shirts that I mentioned earlier, the capote provides a surprising amount of comfort in cold weather. It is not a bulky item and can easily be carried on a back pack rolled in my sleeping blanket. I also like the looks and primitive design of the capote. Plain old jeans are perfect pants for me. For marginal weather, I also suggest long johns. I like a felt hat for trekking. It provides warmth and protection from the sun when needed and is virtually indestructible. My twenty-year-old Stetson has been stomped, soaked, singed, sat on, and shot at, and it has seen more than its share of horse poop. It is just now good and broken in, and though it's an embarrassment in polite society, it should last at least twenty more. A large bandana is a highly versatile article that serves well in all types of emergencies when called upon to do so. Don't leave home without one.

Moccasins just don't cut it except for rendezvous. Like most of the old timers, I wear the best leather boots that I can afford and make sure that they are well broken in before the trip. A recent encounter with a cactus spine in the side of my boot has further convinced me of the importance of good footwear. If in doubt about the weather at all, take along a good pair of gloves. Nothing, and I mean nothing, is worse on these trips than cold hands and feet.

Camp Equipment

For cooking and eating utensils, I recommend a small lightweight boiler, a large tin cup, and a small tin cup, as well as a spoon and fork. One of those handy-dandy Swiss army knives can be thrown in for emergencies. I eat out of the large tin cup, drink from the small cup, and cook in the boiler. I'm just fastidious I guess, but that's the way that I like it.

The only other tools that I usually take along are a small camp saw, a small gardener's hand spade, and that old Queens Steel belt knife that I mentioned in the last chapter. Unless I am going to a primitive campout, I don't like to use a hatchet. The little folding saw is much easier to carry and seems a heck of a lot safer than hacking away with some tomahawk that isn't heavy enough in the first place. The gardener's spade is handy for digging fire pits, trash dumps, and mini-latrines. It doesn't take up nearly the room that even a military shovel does and works well for small jobs. Most importantly, it helps keep things looking the way nature intended.

There are several items that I take trekking that Great-Great-Grandpa didn't. Ziploc baggies are wonderful. They seal up nicely and keep the bug repellent and gun oil off the food. They keep matches and food dry. They protect almost anything that is small enough for them to protect and, combined with a few rubber bands, will even protect the muzzle and lock of your muzzleloader in wet-weather emergencies. Even if your backpack isn't waterproof, these little gems will keep almost everything in your pack dry and useful.

A small flashlight is also taken along, as is toilet paper. You can make up the rest of the story where these two items are concerned. A small first aid kit and water purification tablets also need to be included. A small container of dish or germicidal hand soap will keep you and your eating utensils clean and tidy.

A map, a compass, or a GPS system can be lifesavers in unfamiliar territory. On those evenings that I am camped near a large-enough body of water, I like to set a few bank lines from a small plastic container that I keep in my pack. Once in a while, they supply a tasty addition to breakfast.

Food

For food on the trail, I recommend the usual dehydrated stuff sold in outdoor stores or army surplus field meals. They are light, safe, and sometimes pretty good. Beef jerky will satisfy cravings that granola bars and trail mix don't on the trail. Pour a box of raisin and nut natural cereal into a bag. It is good for you, much more reasonably priced than trail mix, and more filling. It also beats the dickens out of pemmican in all but very cold weather. Instant coffee and tea bags aren't very romantic but it can sure seem that way early in the morning brewed in a tin cup. A coffee pot is really a nuisance in a backpack for no more than it does.

Add these items to your sleeping blankets, rolled in a small canvas, and about fifty feet of quarter-inch sisal or manila hemp rope and you can set yourself up in a comfy little camp. The canvas can be very versatile. By placing .50 or .54 caliber lead balls into the canvas and tying them off from the other side with a rope, effective anchor points for a lean-to or diamond shelter can be created.

Primitive Camping

If you want the challenge of trekking on a more primitive level, there are several fine pack baskets on the market, including one that can be ordered from Dixie. On most models though, you will need to remove the nylon carrying straps and replace them with leather to be strictly authentic. Dixie is also an excellent source for flint strikers, tableware, candle lanterns, and cookware.

Primitive fire-making is quite a challenge, to say the least. It takes patience, determination, and favorable conditions for the making of a fire from scratch the old-fashioned way. A striker or firesteel will be needed. It is usually a C-shaped tool which fits over the knuckles and is struck on flint to create sparks. A piece of old file will work.

Charcloth is used to catch the spark and, if you will, hold the ember until the tinder can be ignited. The best way to make charcloth is to take a small metal container with a very small hole poked in the top and place pieces of cotton (denim jean scraps work best) in it. Heat the container over low heat on your kitchen stove. A small trail of smoke should rise out of the hole indicating that the charcloth is combusting. When the smoke tapers off or quits, remove the container immediately. Plan on ruining several batches before you get it right. Be patient—it will work.

Plains Horsemen—
These horsemen
are typical of
mounted plainsmen.
Authentic horseback
treks provide great
adventure, especially
over the vast open
landscape of the
Plains.

The impatient should try mixing in some plain old clothes dryer lint from your lint trap for combustible material. Nothing works better for flint and steel fire-making if it is dry. I use an old horse salve can for the container, but almost anything will work as long as the lid fits tightly.

Another method of fire-making is to use a magnifying glass to refract sunlight to a point of intensity on your tinder. This works quickly if there is sunlight. There are tobacco boxes with a burning lens mounted in the lid available from Dixie. Dried lawn clippings work very well for tinder. If the weather is cloud, rainy, or moist, it's going to be tough building a fire. This is not a skill for the impatient or easily frustrated. It is also not something that should be tried for the fist time on the trail. Practice making these fires at home before you leave on your trek.

For sleeping blankets, I recommend the eighty percent wool models. One hundred percent wool blankets are expensive and the cheaper models work well. If you are tall, sewing the blankets into a sleeping bag shape will help greatly on cold evenings. Get blankets that are at least 62" by 84". If you can find a larger one, go for it.

As far as cooking is concerned, try cooking over the embers rather than the fire. The food cooks slower but is much less likely to burn or be lost in the flame. So are you. You will find that with practice, you will have quite the multiburner cook stove at your disposal if you allow for small ember piles directly beside your camp fire.

Supply List

A list of those items that you may need for a black powder trek are as follows:

- Rifle, shotgun, and/or pistol
- Black powder or Pyrodex
- Shooting bag with patches, lube, cleaning supplies, and emergency kit
- Short starter and capper
- Hunting knife and stone
- Eating utensils
- Food (stay away from perishable items)
- Canteen and water purification tablets
- Matches or primitive fire tools
- Flashlight or candles

Spanish Molica—The ancestor of the Texas saddle.

- Bedroll and canvas
- Coat or poncho
- Medication and first aid kit
- Toilet tissue
- Rope
- Compass and map
- Camp saw or hatchet
- Bug repellent
- Soap
- Toiletries

If you are going by horseback or boat, you are going to need all the horse and boat items that normally go along with these sports. Better get your horse and yourself familiar with hobbles before the trip so your pony can graze at night. If you're using a boat, get in the habit of securing your gear to the boat or canoe with rope or you may lose much valuable equipment if the boat should capsize.

Finally, don't forget your camera, even if it is cheap. Once you get away from that gasoline engine, you are going to see and hear things that you may have forgotten existed. Trekking will open up a whole new world of nature and fun.

McClellan Saddle—The military saddle of the Indian Wars.

Post-Civil War Saddle—A cowboy saddle that developed in Texas from Spanish stock saddles.

11

Big Game Hunting

THE MOST POPULAR USE OF THE MUZZLE-LOADING RIFLE IN
North America is for big game hunting, primarily the whitetail deer. Special
muzzleloader–only deer seasons have been established for almost all of the states.
Using a primitive, historically correct muzzleloader presents a fine hunting
challenge.

A pair of coyotes taken by the author using a modern Traditions
Yukon in-line rifle.

There are several big game animals that can be hunted with a muzzleloader on the Plains. Black bear and elk are present in small numbers and prevalent in the Rocky Mountains. The whitetail deer, mule deer, and American pronghorn are challenging game animals that will challenge the muzzle-loading hunter's skill. Feral hogs are becoming increasingly popular for muzzleloader hunting, especially as their numbers increase in Texas, Oklahoma, and Kansas. During the time of the Santa Fe Trail there were also great herds of bison. Special bison hunts can be arranged with private outfitters in several plains states.

Whitetail Deer

Although spread throughout the forty-eight contiguous states and easily the most plentiful big game animal in the country, whitetail deer were not the most plentiful game on the Plains in the old days. The Plains environment did not provide

Kansas' early season muzzle-loader deer season is often warm with a lot of cover. This is perfect for hunting with a big-bore, open-sight muzzleloader.

the ideal habitat for a browser of the brush and thick country. Whitetail populations began rebuilding in the 20th century because of a much-altered Plains region. The enormous expanse of open range land became a land of modern agriculture. With the growth of farming, prairie fires that once kept the land free of brush and trees ceased to exist. Groves of trees along waterways, in shelter belts, and in over-grazed pasture survived under man's influence and so did the whitetail population.

As recently as forty years ago in my area of central Kansas, seeing a whitetail deer was an unusual experience. A state deer season did not exist in Kansas until the middle of the 1960s. Since that time deer have expanded their population to such a level that they are considered a common driving hazard. Farmers complain of the crop damage done by deer. The opening of deer season now rivals Kansas's pheasant season for involvement and interest.

In 1989, Kansas began a muzzleloader-only deer season usually timed in the middle of September. Since summer foliage is still heavy, the September muzzleloader-only whitetail season is normally a short-range endeavor. Deer hunting is normally limited to narrow bands of trees and brush. Hunting from a blind or tree stand in the very early and very late hours of daylight is most productive. Shots are seldom more than a hundred yards. Kansas allows only mechanical sights on muzzleloaders for the early season so there is very little if any advantage to hunting with an in-line.

Whitetail deer tend to remain within a mile or two of their prime habitat and they like to move close to cover. Finding deer trails and setting up on them is a far more productive strategy than still hunting at this time of year.

Fast handling carbines are especially effective during the early season, especially sidelock muzzleloaders that are easy to maneuver in the blind. Patch round balls of .45 caliber or larger are effective for whitetail deer. I prefer a big .50 caliber conical of at least 385 grains to create heavy blood trails. An accurate sidelock muzzleloader is ideal for mid-September deer hunting.

Mule Deer

Mule deer offer a much different challenge for the muzzle-loading hunter. Mule deer move extensively and position themselves in open areas. While this tactic works against them when pressed by the hunter using a scope-mounted .30-06 or .270, it is extremely effective against the black powder hunter. Using a spotting scope or binoculars, a hunter will need to locate the mule deer and then try to move up on them without being spotted. It can be quite a challenge.

In rougher country I have often successfully taken mule deer using a technique called canyon jumping. By being familiar with the area and having conducted pre-season scouting, I move up on a canyon where I believe mule deer may be resting during the day. Taking the prevailing wind into account, stalk the canyon as you would the deer. If your are lucky and have guessed correctly you will often catch mule deer lounging on the sides of the canyon and get a shot before they are aware of you. Mulies often lounge in the sun on colder days, using the canyons for protection. The first and largest mule deer buck I took with a muzzleloader was taken in this fashion. The deer were watching another group of hunters moving down a canyon below them and were distracted. The challenges of hunting in this fashion are great but the rewards and feelings of accomplishment are even greater.

Mule deer can be taken with .45 caliber or larger round ball loads. Range is often at least a hundred yards and you need a good straight shooting rifle with fine open or receiver sights. I prefer a .50 caliber rifle for mule deer.

Feral Hogs and Javelina

Feral hog numbers are rapidly increasing and it is a very good hunting bargain if you are a meat hunter. I normally hunt hogs in Texas every spring. I set up on water holes and feeding areas and wait for them to come in. Feral hogs can be easily stalked if the wind is right because they do not have good eyesight. By walking straight at them while they are feeding or drinking, I have often been able to get within thirty yards of them. I like a .50 or .54 muzzleloader for feral hogs. They can easily be taken with round balls or conicals. I prefer the additional knockdown powder of a heavy conical from 400 to 435 grains in weight.

Javelina can also be easily stalked as well as called with a javelina call. Do not be surprised if javelina retreat before gathering together and coming back to the sound of a stressed javelina. A .45 caliber round ball can take javelina because they are not difficult to bring down. I always carry a backup revolver when calling javelina with a muzzleloader as they can be quite aggressive when riled and more than one shot may be necessary to turn a pack of them.

American Pronghorn Antelope

Hunting the American pronghorn with a muzzleloader is a challenge. Pronghorns possess eyesight that rivals eight power binoculars, a nervous disposition, and the fastest sustained speed of any land animal in the world. The pronghorn is the product of twenty million years of evolution on the open plains and is unique to the world. He was defeated by the advent of the barbed wire fence and the high-powered, long-range rifle. His numbers were second only to the bison. During the 1870s and 1880s market hunters dealt the pronghorn population a serious blow, profiting from an exchange rage of three carcasses for twenty-five cents. This killing was accomplished by breech loading single shots such as the Springfield, Sharps, and Remington. Pronghorns taken by muzzleloaders in the early years were usually the inexperienced or animals that were blundered upon by travelers along the trails. Today, the pronghorn exists on the eastern slopes of the Rockies in Colorado,

Taking an American pronghorn with a muzzleloader is a major hunting challenge.

New Mexico, Wyoming, and Montana. He can also be found farther out on the plains of the Dakotas, Nebraska, Texas, and Kansas, but in small numbers. His one disadvantage is his immense curiosity, which may draw him toward a hunter that he does not recognize as a threat. Otherwise the pronghorn is a challenging target for a muzzleloader.

A .45 caliber round ball will take a pronghorn but I prefer a .50 with a light conical to help with distance and wind drift. Perhaps one of the best muzzleloader shots I ever took was at a young pronghorn buck at 206 paces. I was very lucky to make the shot with open sights.

Black Bear and Elk

Big game hunting with a muzzleloader is not difficult as long as the hunter can close the range. I like to shoot both black bear and elk at closer ranges of under

100 yards with a big conical of over 400 grains. A .50 will do the job but a .54 will do it so much better. So much better, in fact, that my newest big game muzzleloader is a .58 caliber Leman plains rifle replica.

I took a nice cow elk with a .58 caliber Civil War replica carbine at forty yards using a 525-grain conical and seventy grains of black powder. I spined her and she collapsed so suddenly that we had to roll her off her legs folded beneath her to begin field dressing. It was a very impressive performance.

On my only black bear hunt I did not connect but my hunting partner shot a nice boar with a .54 shooting a 435-grain conical at fifty yards. The bear rolled, regained his footing, and traveled less than twenty yards before going down. I was standing beside my partner ready to put a .58 conical in him if he turned on us. I didn't need to shoot. The .54 did very well.

Gun Recommendations

Most big game animals are best pursued by a hunter armed with a .45, .50, .54, or .58 muzzleloader loaded with a heavy conical. I do not trust a conventional .45 sidelock shooting a round ball for anything larger than a deer. However, a .45 loaded with a heavy conical is very effective on all big game. I have hunted Asian

Powder Measure—Always use a powder measure to load a gun and never pour directly from the horn.

Charge Your Powder—Pour the powder from the measure into the rifle bore. Slap the side of the rifle gently to settle the powder.

buffalo, African plains game, and North American game with a .50 loaded with 385- to 600-grain conicals and was always quite satisfied. A .58 is generally considered a short-range gun because of its slow speed and rainbow trajectory, but for the big animals I love a .58. A .54 is a very practical sidelock big game caliber. A .54 caliber round ball gun is effective on hogs, deer, and javelina. That same gun loaded with a standard 435-grain conical is just as effective on larger game. The sidelock .54 has fallen out of favor in the popular media because it is compared to .50 caliber in-line sabot rifles. That is too bad because all my experiences have demonstrated to me that a .54 caliber sidelock rifle is far more effective on big game than it is given credit for and just as devastating on big game as any .50 caliber sabot load.

If you are purchasing a sidelock for hunting, pay attention to the rifling twist. A slow twist of 1:60" or 1:66" is best for round ball loads. A moderate twist rate of 1:48," 1:38," or 1:32" is best for conicals. A 1:48" (one full turn in forty-eight inches of length) is the best compromise twist rate. Most .54 rifles have 1:48" twist rates.

No Plains state restricts the hunter to a flintlock, so a percussion rifle is the better choice for the beginner. Practice extensively at reloading your muzzleloader without breaking your silhouette. It will prove to be the second most valuable skill that you can employ behind simple accurate shooting. I have often been able to reload my rifle without alarming big game after a shot by not breaking my outline toward them.

Elements for Success

Four basic elements for success apply for the muzzle-loading hunter on the Plains. They may sound simple but each is vital.

First, know your weapon. To be successful, the hunter must be totally familiar with the range and limitations of his rifle. Simply sighting the rifle as a predetermined distance is not enough, although it is mandatory for beginning. Because of the varying wind and range conditions of the Plains, the hunter must practice often and keep mental notes of how his rifle functions.

Target shooting from the hilltops and bottoms of canyons that he intends to hunt will pay valuable dividends. I have dictated to myself that my range limit for most shots is 120 yards with open sights, but the vast majority of my muzzleloader shot attempts are less than 100 yards. I stick to that range because I know my shooting ability and am not proficient with open sights beyond that range. I consider it irresponsible for me to take a shot beyond that range unless it is under very special-

Short Starter—After centering the patch and ball over the bore, use a short starter to drive the ball into the bore and allow the soft lead ball to engage the rifling.

ized conditions (sun on the target, no wind, a solid brace to shoot from, and still game). I am generally thought of by those I hunt with as a good shot, but that is because I don't take risky shots and therefore do not miss as often in the field. I don't take shots at running game unless it is a direct crossing or quartering shot, I can easily judge the pace, and the range is short. Actually, I am an average shot with a conservative shooting philosophy. Just as good.

Second, know your equipment. Once the shot is taken, it is important for the muzzleloader hunter to be totally familiar with his tools and equipment. Fumbling for a short starter, ball, or patch and not having success can rattle the most experienced shooter. Whether the shooter decides on a redi-load, loading block, shooting bag, or powder horn, he needs to be totally familiar with the location of every item that he is using. Decide on the methods and equipment, then stick with them until totally comfortable and confident. It will go a long way toward improving both shooting and hunting. I can reload both of my main hunting sidelocks from the bag without ever looking at my rifle. I have separate shooting bags for each rifle with different loading equipment for each. The only common element I carry is my bison powder horn.

Ram Rod—Use a ram rod to drive the ball up to and directly against the powder charge. Notice that the author is taking short strokes on the rod so as not to put undo pressure on the wood and cause the rod to snap.

Capper—A capper is not necessary but it does save time and helps with manipulation of the cap in cold weather. Capping the nipple with a percussion cap is the last step before cocking and firing the rifle.

Third, know your game. Riding around in a pickup truck hoping to blunder upon a deer may work fine for the fellow using a modern rifle, but it spells failure for the muzzleloader hunter. The muzzleloader hunter needs to scout his prey, know its habits, know the area, and use his best judgment. This means making a greater hunting effort to know where the game is and what it will probably do. It is part of the challenge and reward of muzzle-loading.

Last, know yourself. Buying a muzzle-loading rifle is the same as making a commitment to yourself that you are willing to accept the handicaps as well as the rewards of muzzle-loading. If taking game is your primary motivation, then it is probably not a sport that you should attempt. There are going to be many times that the experience is all that you are going to have to show for your efforts.

The muzzleloader hunter will need to take more time, pass up more shots, and brace for failures than the modern equipped hunter. It can be frustrating at time, but it can also be enormously rewarding. I have seen many fine muzzle-loading rifles traded in after only one season because the hunter was not willing to pay the price that it takes to be successful. Be aware of and be willing to face the odds that you are placing upon yourself and hunting with modern arms may simply lose its appeal.

Starter Load Recommendations

These are recommended loads to begin with in your search for a proper load for big game. Start with a low load and test your gun for accuracy by working up in five-grain increments. It is wise to note that the largest load is never the best load. Muzzleloader accuracy is far more important than raw power. These are estimated loads using a 28" barrel. Velocity and muzzle energy increase with barrel length. A 36" barrel in a .45 caliber rifle with a 70-grain load will almost equal a .50 caliber rifle with a 28" barrel and 80-grain load. Larger calibers enjoy greater projectile weight for greater momentum to improve the advantage over smaller calibers as distance increases.

Caliber	Charge	FPS	Muzzle energy (ft.-lbs.)	100 Yard Energy (ft.-lbs.)
.45 ball	60 grs.	1,585	741	245
133 grains	70 grs.	1,670	822	260
.45 conical	50 grs.	1,335	908	436
230 grains	60 grs.	1,532	1,196	504
.50 ball	70 grs.	1,663	1,104	389
180 grains	80 grs.	1,777	1,260	424
.54 ball	80 grs	1,270	1,323	708
220 grains	90 grs.	1,388	940	413
.54 proj.	80 grs.	1,136	1,173	815
410 grains	90 grs.	1,278	1,458	947

Do not be deceived by what seems to be unimpressive figures. These loads are very effective on light-boned game such as deer out to a range of 100 yards.

12

Muzzleloader Shotgun Hunting

IN SPITE OF WHAT HAS BEEN WRITTEN IN THE MEDIA, MY NOMI-
nation for the gun that won the West is the common shotgun. The United States
may be a nation of riflemen, but it was the shotgun that was called upon to do first
duty as a provider of game for the table and defender of the family. Shotguns were
formidable and deadly when loaded with buck and ball. Shotguns were available
to the general public at low cost and when the going got tough, they would shoot
almost anything a pioneer had to shove down the barrel.

The muzzle–loading shotgun has lagged behind the rifle during the rebirth of
black powder. Replica scattergun choices are not nearly those of the rifle. This is
unfortunate because, while the black powder rifle lags behind modern rifle ballis-
tics, the properly loaded percussion shotgun will rival modern shotguns in the field.
Only the time involved in loading is the muzzleloader's weakness.

The muzzleloader shotgun's loading process presents a new opportunity for the
shooter who desires more challenge. I've found that my wing shooting has actually
improved with a muzzleloader. Knowing that I do not have backup rounds, I have
taken a split second longer to properly point and lead the gun and passed up many
marginal shots. This has greatly improved my first hit success rate.

Muzzle-Loading Shotgun Selections

In the early years of the rebirth of muzzle-loading several companies offered
excellent sidelock percussion and flintlock shotguns. Since there have never been
special muzzleloader-only upland game, waterfowl, and varmint seasons, these shot-

guns never sold in numbers approaching the rifles. Many of these models are still available on the used gun market and often in pristine condition.

Thompson/Center sold a nice percussion single shot called the New Englander. It was available with either a walnut or weather-resistant Rynite stock. This was my first muzzleloader shotgun because of price and availability. I hunted with one for several seasons. It was quick to point and dependable. Its size makes it an excellent choice for a small-framed shooter.

CVA marketed a Trapper single-shot sidelock shotgun equipped with inter-changeable chokes. Its balance and handling were quite similar to the New Eng-lander. Mowrey's Ethan Allen 12 gauge single-shot was an unusual shotgun that appealed to the eye and the pocketbook. It is a dependable shotgun.

Dixie Gun Company still sells the Mortimer flint shotgun. It is a 12 gauge with a 36" barrel and it is a beautiful piece to handle and admire.

. Today the black powder sidelock shotgun market is dominated by the Davide Pedersoli percussion double barrel. This gun is sold by nearly all the black powder marketers. Some double-barrel black power shotgun models feature chrome-lined barrels for use with steel shot. Some 10 and 12 gauge models use screw-in choke

Cabela's Double—The author has carried this Cabela's 12 gauge double-barrel percussion shotgun for fifteen years. With proper care and regular maintenance, this gun will last a lifetime.

tubes for greater flexibility and come with X-Full, modified, and improved cylinder chokes. The 20 gauge has a fixed improved cylinder and a fixed modified choke. This shotgun had deep, slick bluing, engraved locks and checkered American walnut stocks.

I have owned and hunted with a Davide Pedersoli 12 gauge double for fifteen years. I have worn out one set of locks and had to have them rebuilt. It has proven to be an excellent turkey, varmint, and upland game gun. I have not hunted waterfowl with it but it is designed for steel shot.

The problem I always had with the single-barrel shotguns was for pheasant and turkey hunting. There were situations especially when a pheasant was flying straight away from me and that one shot was not enough to bring the bird down. I needed that second shot that a single barrel couldn't supply. There were also a couple of times when my load misfired on turkeys and an instant second shot would have been the difference between taking and losing a Tom. When I switched to my Pedersoli double, those problems were eliminated.

Those who want an authentic replica of the most common scattergun on the early plains should look for a flintlock Northwest Trade Gun in 12, 20, or 24 gauges. This was the all-purpose weapon of the Indian and the early plainsman. Its popularity is evident by the fact that it was commonly marketed in the early 20th century to Canadian Indians and Eskimos.

A beginner should consider a percussion shotgun over a flintlock. The delayed firing reaction of the flint gun demands skill and patience for accurate shooting. I often hunt with Dr. Gary White, who uses a flintlock shotgun for turkeys. Doc has often demonstrated that a good, well-tuned flintlock shotgun is just as quick on ignition as any percussion or in-line gun with virtually no delay. He uses guns that he has made himself and is an expert on touchhole and pan alignment. He is fastidious about flint maintenance. Most beginners are not and do not have access to a finely crafted flintlock smoothbore. A good trade gun is the way to start down that road.

Keep It Simple!

One of the reasons for the muzzle-loading shotgun not enjoying the popularity of the rifle is that many potential buyers are concerned about what seems to be complicated loading procedures. Buyers hear of ounces versus drams and grains, overshot wads, and overpowder wads. It seems complicated and slow.

This does injustice to a very simple and efficient gun. Do like the old-timers did and keep it simple. Most of you will never know the difference if you follow some simple advice about shotgunning.

First of all, the terminology of ounces of shot, drams of powder, and grains of powder is confusing. A dram of powder is equal in volume to 27 ½ grains of powder in a rifle. Call it 27 or 26 and forget about it. The measurement of ounces of shot refers to the weight of shot for individual loads.

The easiest solution is to load a shotgun on a one-to-one ration for game or when you begin patterning. A good 12 gauge upland load is ninety grains of #6 shot over niney grains of FFg black powder. I am referring to volume amounts that are measued with a common measuring device. A one-to-one ration is easy to remember and just as effective as anything else you can dream up.

I use Federal half-inch thick 12-gauge cushion fiber wads in front of both shot and powder and have never experienced a blown pattern. Normally I will split the overshot wad with my thumbnail but it is not necessary. Overshot cards are fragile and difficult to align properly past tight chokes. When chokes are especially tight I often use a short starter to force the wads past them. I keep my fiber wads loose in my loading bag so that I do not have to fumble for a specific kind. It greatly speeds reloading time.

You can have too much of a good thing when shotgunning. Guys are always trying to develop "Magnum" loads for turkey hunting and end up with terrible patterns from hard-recoiling powder charges. Ninety grains of powder and an equal volume of shot for a 12 gauge, eighty-five grains for a 16 gauge, and seventy-five grains for a 20 gauge are excellent field loads and easy to gauge and remember.

Support Equipment—Managing powder, shot charges, and caps demands for minimum support equipment. Shown are shot snake and charger, powder measure, nipple pick, capper, and shot wads.

You'll get a bigger boom with more powder and shot but little else. Keep your loads simple and moderate and you will enjoy successful shooting.

I prefer #5 shot for turkeys, #6 shot for most pheasant, small game, and quail, and #7 ½ for morning doves. If you don't have interchangeable chokes, you can use a plastic shot collar wad to increase pattern density. I have often done this for turkey and coyote hunting but not for upland game or rabbits because it slows the loading process.

Make certain that your loads are well packed and remain that way. Loads can work loose, especially with a double barrel that is being shot a great deal with one barrel and not the other. It is also a good idea to cover the barrel you are not load-ing to help prevent double loading. I generally pull my ramrod and rest it in the unfired muzzle while loading.

Never load a double barrel with the percussion cap still on the unshot barrel. When I load two barrels at a time, I always charge the left barrel first. There is no reason for that other than developing the habit of doing things the same way every time, which is important for safe shooting.

Backup Supplies

For years I carried my shot in one horn and my powder in another and used the same measure for both. There are a number of shot pouches on the market if a horn doesn't interest you. Many of them have attached premeasured scoops and chargers. This will save reloading time. My current bag has a shot pouch attached to the shoulder strap with a shot charger.

Many suggest using premeasured charges. This will save bulk and time. It is a very effective practice for turkey or coyote hunting where you don't expect a lot of shooting. For a day afield, however, I prefer a shooting bag and shot snake.

Tips for Successful Shotgunning

In order to overcome the disadvantage of only having one or two immediate shots, develop the practice of holding your position and carefully reloading before taking another step, especially when hunting upland game. I have often flushed a pheasant or covey of quail, knocked birds down, reloaded on the spot, advanced with a freshly charged load, and brought up another bird with the next step. Getting two birds from the same area with a single-shot muzzleloader is not a pipe dream. It can be regularly done, especially in cold weather when the birds are less likely to run or fly. The shooter needs to develop an deliberate attitude and control his actions. This is the challenge of muzzle-loading. Taking a large number of birds is not the idea. Even a single-shot cartridge shotgun will reload much quicker than a muzzleloader. It is the challenge of muzzle-loading that is the appeal. Once you develop that attitude, you will be surprised at how many birds you will take.

T/C New Englander—A single-barrel muzzleloader such as this Thompson/Center New Englander 12 gauge is an excellent small game, turkey, and small bird hunter. It falls short where backup shots are necessary.

Pheasant

The king of the game birds on the Plains is the Chinese Ringneck pheasant. They are an import from China and do very well in mixed agricultural and grazing lands. The bird is hunted by flushing him from cover. He is slow to take off and usually noisy. He is perfect for beginning muzzleloaders because he is relatively easy to find and shoot. And if you haven't had pheasant and noodles, then you just haven't eaten! The season is from early fall through the end of January. Hunting is best when it is cold or snowy and the birds are holding tight. They are most active in the late morning, early afternoons, and early evening. Hunting is usually best during the very early morning when the birds are warm and do not want to leave their positions. Try heavy cover nest to harvested fields of grain, fence rows, waterways, and weedy fields for best luck. I recommend a 12 gauge using ninety grains of powder and from #4 to #6 shot of equal volume. As the season progresses and the birds become wilder, the heavier shot will do better at longer ranges.

Quail

Bobwhite and scaled quail make for excellent hunting in the West. These are small birds that move in coveys of six to twenty. These little guys prefer thick brush and plenty of cover. The best shooting technique is to pick up one bird with your sight point and stay with him until you shoot. If you don't you are liable to find yourself shooting wildly in confusion. Don't feel too bad if you get rattled when flushing the first few coveys. It happens to most of us.

This is my favorite muzzleloader upland bird. Where pheasant hunting is usually done with a large group of hunters who want to keep shooting lines even, quail hunting is perfect for a single hunter and a good dog. I often feel pressured by others to reload quickly when pheasant hunting but that is not the case on a cold Saturday in December and January when everyone else is watching the ball game and I am out alone with my dog. There is an almost leisurely aspect to muzzle-loading for quail in spite of the ruckus of a covey rise.

Walking the edges of waterways and dry streams will produce good populations, especially when near thick brush. A 12 gauge load of #7 ½ shot and eighty grains of powder is a good quail choice. I usually use #6 shot and ninety grains of powder because of the likelihood of also flushing the occasional pheasant.

Doves

Morning dove hunting is good for the shooting skills but not so great for the frustration level. The little gray flyers are fast and fleeting. They are a migrating bird that is hunting in the late summer and early fall before the weather forces them further south. In the western plains you will have the most success in the early morning and late evening when the birds come to water. Shelter belts next to windmills and ponds are excellent spots for hunting doves. Plan on quite a bit of shooting before you get very many. It is great fun and a good way to sharpen the shooting eye before the later bird seasons. Use a light load of seventy grains of powder and an equal amount of #7 ½ shot.

Prairie Chicken

There are only five states that allow prairie chicken hunting. Kansas has the largest population and its season usually is timed with pheasant and quail seasons. Prairie chickens are about the same size as pheasants but they are much faster and fly higher. They must have a habitat that is at least thirty percent open grassland to flourish. A good hunting method is behind cover on the edges of fields during the morning and evening and pass shoot as the birds work from grass to grain.

The more common method is to flush them from tall grass. Be prepared for the possibility of a great deal of walking with sporadic success. Try to locate populations by scouting and stalk them early in the morning. Prairie chickens are fast and wary, and the open grassland is their perfect environment. They are excellent table fare. A ninety-grain powder charge and equal measure of #5 or #6 shot is my suggested load.

Turkey

I have read chronicles of the early Santa Fe Trail that told of inexperienced hunters mistaking great flocks of turkey for their first bison sightings. It must have been a sight to behold. I did not see a turkey in the wild in Kansas until about thirty years ago. They had been virtually wiped out on the plains by the turn of the twentieth century. Their numbers have increased steadily since reintroduction in the 1960s.

The turkey is the Plains game management success story, second only to the whitetail deer. These birds are wary survivors and probably the greatest game bird challenge on the Plains today. They prefer the river bottom overgrowth but can be found in well-watered valleys. The turkey hunter must conceal himself and use calls to try to lure the old Toms into range. Camouflage clothing is an advantage for turkey hunters. Hunting these birds demands a lot of preseason scouting to determine where the birds are roosting. A great variety of calls are available. Pick your call and practice, as this is one effort that will take skill and patience. A box call is necessary to counter the winds of spring. A hunter needs his call to be recognizable up to a mile on the Plains.

Too many hunters call too much. Once a turkey responds to the call, wait several minutes before calling again. Calling too often makes it easy for the birds to spot your position and it does not entice the bird to come toward you except in certain circumstances. I've witnessed too many hunters immediately respond to a gobble with a call without waiting for them to close the distance. Henned-up gobblers will be very vocal and not come in. Better to wait until later in the day when the hens have broken off contact.

Breeding season for Rio Grandes can be very short on the Plains, so it is often necessary to establish ambuscades. Glassing from ridge tops and moving into posi-

Muzzleloader Turkey—This nice Rio Grande was taken at thirty yards using the Cabela's double with the right barrel choked full and the left choked extra full with standard pheasant load of 90 grains of FFg and an equal volume measure of #6 shot. The right barrel was used and the left barrel held in reserve for a longer shot or a misfire.

tion as turkeys pass along narrow creek channels is a very effective strategy. Decoys can also be very good for distracting turkeys as cover is often slight in these areas.

I recommend #2 or #4 shot over at least 100 grains of black powder in a gauge. A 10 gauge is not out of line for these birds. Use a full or extra full choke and plastic shot collars to tighten your pattern. I have killed turkeys at 50 paces using muzzle-loading shotguns with guns that patterned as tightly as any modern gun, and with less recoil. A muzzle-loading shotgun is ideal for turkey hunting. Use a fresh load each day to reduce the chances of a misfire.

Waterfowl

Modern Hevi-shot and tungsten shot have changed muzzle-loading for ducks and geese into a fine pursuit. A good 12- or 10-gauge double-choked full and extra full with a load of 100 grains of black powder and an equal volume of #4 shot is my normal choice for ducks. I use #2 shot for geese. A Pedersoli shotgun recommended for steel shot will do well with BB steel shot and 100 grains of FFg black powder. Use plastic shot collars to extend range and pattern density if you do not have chokes.

I recommend a 10 gauge for ducks and geese if they are your primary hunting goals. I like the extra shot a 10 gauge offers in its loads. Try to shoot from a blind where you can reload easily from a standing or sitting position, as muzzleloaders do not do well with prone loading positions.

An eastern gobbler taken by the author with a Traditions in-line muzzleloading shotgun. This 12-gauge is capable of 40- to 50-yard shots.

13

Varmints and Small Game

COYOTES AND PRAIRIE DOGS ARE MOST SUCCESSFULLY HUNTED with modern small-caliber, high-velocity rifles. Putting a coyote down at 200 yards or a prairie dog at 100-plus yards is a job for a rifle that did not exist in the early West. Old-timers hunted the coyote as well as the prairie dog. Indians counted them as good food.

If you want to test your muzzle-loading shooting skills, then varminting may be your challenge. In my state coyotes, prairie dogs, and rabbits can be hunted year-round. They are small targets and difficult at long range because of muzzleloader trajectory.

Wolves

During the days of the Santa Fe Trail there was a creature knows as the buffalo or lobo wolf on the Plains. I don't want to belabor the point of just how big and bad these fellows were, but all one needs to examine is the huge size of a bison to recognize how big and bad these wolves must have been. Even in a sick and weakened condition, a mature bison was difficult for any creature to take down. Lobo wolves followed the herds year-round and probably made a good living by scavenging off the leavings of the herd. Yet there are stories of packs dragging down by these formidable beasts. But the lobo is no more. After the extermination of the buffalo, the lobo turned to the white man's livestock and was shot into extinction by the 1930s.

Because of the successful reintroduction of wolves, regulated hunting may again become a reality. I would want at least a .50 caliber rifle for such a hunt.

Coyotes

Replacing wolves on the Plains was little *Canis latrans*, the coyote. Probably no other animal has been so romantically associated with the Old West and at the same time so frequently cursed by farmers and ranchers. What western scene would be complete without the coyote's howl keeping the cowboys company as they gather around the campfire? It is still that way on the Plains. The trouble is that it is also that way in suburban Los Angeles and Denver as well. The coyote's range has spread into western North America from the Arctic Ocean to Mexico, eastward to James Bay, Quebec, Vermont, and the Mississippi River, south to New Orleans, and east to Florida. Coyotes are tough adversaries.

This Ruger 77-50 in-line muzzleloader was set up exclusively for coyote hunting.

I've used sidelocks for coyotes. Of merit were a custom .45 caliber Ohio rifle, a .54 caliber Lyman Deerstalker equipped with Lyman peep sights, and a .50 caliber Traditions Hawken Woodsman. All of these rifles could group inside of three inches using round ball loads and moderate powder charges of 70 to 90 grains. The .54 Lyman did best using Buffalo Ball-ets, as the .32 and .36 caliber round ball guns did not put coyotes down with the authority that I prefer. Coyotes always travel several yards after impact from the .45 round ball rifle. A .50 round ball sidelock possesses a nice combination of flat shooting trajectory and lethality. The .54 Lyman worked so well because of its sights and the excellent performance of the Buffalo Ball-et in that caliber.

Because only one shot is available, a coyote-calling muzzleloader needs to be very accurate and dependable. I prefer black powder for sidelock coyote hunting to insure ignition. A scoped in-line will extend your credible range on coyotes out to a hundred and fifty yards. Standard sabot deer loads have a shallow trajectory, more energy at long distance, and do more internal damage than round balls. A .50 caliber in-line shooting a 260-grain sabot is nearly perfect for coyotes.

In spite of the in-line advantage, a traditional round ball gun is very effective out to a hundred and twenty yards if it has an accurate load. For close-range woods calling, a .54 or .50 sidelock is fast on target and will put your dog down for keeps. A scope or a peep sight always improves you success ratio.

A beginner needs to master three basic mouth calls. An open reed howler is used for location work and for short barks to stop a coyote. A good closed reed distress call is used for most of your calling. As Gerry Blair is famous for saying, "Put lots of blood in the call." Don't blow too loud. Go for drama over volume. Finally, a good coaxer will come in handy often enough that you probably should have one. I have one nice unit that is a combination call—coaxer on one end, distress cry on the other. Hang them on a lanyard around your neck so that they are quickly and easily accessible.

Electronic calls do a nice job if you hunt often enough to justify the expense of one. The small handheld units are best for close work and practically worthless for anything else. I have a Loman Invisi-Predator wireless unit. I like it for heavy woods calling and as a distraction when coyotes come in. I normally hang it thirty yards to my left (I am right-handed) and use it to draw the coyote's attention away from my location for a shot. Digital calls are nice and they are expensive. They do a good job. I still prefer a cassette player because I have a number of season-specific calls that I consider better sounding, and it is paid for. An electronic call is especially nice if you are hunting alone because you can watch the immediate area more carefully.

I keep my electronic and mouth calls in a shoulder strap "calling bag" and usu-ally always have it in the truck. A flashlight, facemask, gloves, extra batteries, and loads are also kept in the bag.

Camouflage clothing helps but most important are a face mask and gloves. I am a firm believer that coyotes can make out the color blue, so I usually avoid wearing blue jeans in favor of tan, black, or brown. Just as when turkey hunting, the best strategy is to break up your outline for a set and keep movement to an absolute minimum. Binoculars are simply too important a tool to justify leaving behind.

An inexpensive plastic spray bottle charged with one part coon scent and ten parts water can be sprayed liberally into the air when calling in heavy woods and for masking human scent after laying down bait. This is called "misting" and I believe it is absolutely necessary in most muzzleloader-range situations.

In spite of all this equipment, a caller needs to move in as quickly and quietly as possible. Hide your truck from easy view. I've always had my best luck when I got to my calling site well before sunrise, received an answer from a howl inquiry, waited until it was just light enough to see, and then called. Call from where you think they travel and eat in the morning and evening. Call over resting places, water sources, and heavy cover during midday. I usually glass from a height at midday and, if I see a coyote, attempt a stalk or call. In the right area this can be very effective and is an underrated strategy. If you sit still and keep quiet, you'll be surprised at the number of coyotes you'll see at midday.

Hunters with limited access to land need to consider baiting as a tool to develop and reinforce coyote travel patterns. Regular placement of roadkills, expired meat, and even table scraps get the coyote on a regular buffet schedule. Setting up over yesterday's deer intestines and hide during deer season is a way to add spice and coyotes to your hunting season. I normally cover this type of bait to discourage smaller predators and vultures. I use turkey, feral hog, and pheasant carcasses during the seasons and rabbits year-round. For bait to be effective it has to be seasoned and develop a fine stench. For this reason, many refrain from using it. The next best form of bait is a feed yard, lambing, or calving area. A freshly dead large animal always means a coyote will be near that night and early the next morning, if there are any in the area. Dairy, hog, and chicken farms are coyote magnets.

Time your hunt and develop strategies to best fit the coyote's yearly cycle of life. Use puppy in distress calls and fawn bleats in the spring and summer. Use territorial challenge calls from late February through April to take advantage of mating season. Use the rabbit distress call year-round, but it will be most effective in the fall to take inexperienced pups and in the hard winter to take stressed coyotes.

The major advantage to hunting coyotes with a muzzleloader is that once you've mastered taking them, all forms of big game muzzleloader hunting seem much easier. When you have a muzzleloader that you can nail a thirteen- to twenty-pound coyote with at a hundred yards, shooting big game with that same gun is a breeze. Your kill zone goes from salad plate size on a coyote to dinner plate size on big game and you'll not be nearly as likely to buy into the 150-grain powder charge argument. You'll know exactly what you can do with a properly "load-balanced" muzzleloader and realize its importance for big game hunting over raw velocity claims.

You'll also come to realize what an effective medium-range hunting rifle a muzzleloader can be and you'll be more successful in all forms of muzzleloader hunting. A lot of what you've been told about the capabilities of a muzzleloader will be either proven or disproved. Coyote hunting helps you develop stalking skills, animal behavior knowledge, shooting distance judgment, and your shooting skills.

I've hunted on three continents with a muzzleloader and learned more about muzzle-loading while coyote hunting than any other single activity. I know I am a better hunter because I hunt coyotes with a muzzleloader. Try it.

Prairie Dogs

A .45 muzzleloader excels when shooting prairie dogs out to fifty or sixty yards, but these rodents almost disappear behind open sights beyond that. There may have been 800 million prairie dogs living on the plains before the white man settled. Dog towns 200 miles long and twenty miles wide have been documented. Some travelers ate prairie dogs, but I have not read in anyone's journal that they particularly enjoyed them. They appear to have a heavy, earthy flavor according to journals I have read. Early travelers made do with what was available because fresh meat of any kind was highly valued. The praire dog has been pushed into isolated areas, but they are still a common sight on the Plains.

Feral Hogs

Feral hogs are nearly perfect game for a muzzleloader hunter. Most of the feral hogs I've seen in West Texas weigh less than 400 pounds. I've taken feral hogs weighing from as light as sixty pounds to as heavy as 500. The best eating size—food is the main reason I hunt them—is from 100 to 300 pounds. I've had hogs respond to a rabbit distress call and a M.A.D. bleating fawn in cold weather. We have not had much luck in warmer conditions.

During a Texas hog hunt in March, temperatures were approaching 90 degrees. I set up an ambush over a water hole and took several hogs from 4:00 PM to sundown.

My personal preference for muzzle-loading in this circumstance is for a heavy conical weighing at least 400 grains, but a round ball load in .45, .50, .54, or .58 will take hogs easily. The heavy conical will not tear up a coyote badly and still has the power to take a hog.

I recently heard a guide comment that the feral hog is the poor man's Cape buffalo. I was amused by his statement because I tend to approach hog hunting that way. I prefer shoulder shots that "break" hogs down on the spot. They are tough critters, and my preference is to do the most initial damage I can with the first shot.

Tracking a wounded hog, while not particularly dangerous, is often frustrating, as they don't usually leave much of a blood trail and they can go quite a distance with a mortal wound. During dry seasons, most of the time in West Texas, they don't leave good tracks in the hard-packed soil and tend to follow well-used trails, which further confuses tracking. I am not comfortable hunting hogs with any muzzle-loading projectile that weighs in at less than 300 grains. Most of my shots are taken within 100 yards, with the vast majority within 50 yards.

In the West Texas Palo Duro canyon country and along the Pease River, I spend most of my day glassing from the tops of high ridges at several hundred yards over open fields and feeding areas. If a hog presents itself, I try to stalk as close a possible before taking a shot. Stalking through mesquite is not a complicated process. I'll close the distance to within 100 yards or so and then stand erect, wearing camouflage and often a face mask. I concentrate on watching the hog I'm stalking very closely. I advance from downwind taking no more than three steps at a time. If the hog looks up, I freeze in position and wait for him to go back to foraging. I walk directly for him and do not weave, duck, or dive behind cover. Usually, I can get within thirty or forty yards and put him down for good with one shot to the point of the shoulder. Does it work? I've taken seven hogs in seven hunting trips using this system. It's a lot more work than the other styles of hunting, but it is pure enjoyment testing your stalking skills to the maximum. I tried using a bipod on one Texas hunt but did not have good luck. Most of the time it was in the way for that style of hunting. A bipod also does not work very well for coyote shooting in thick mesquite where most of my shot opportunities have been closer than 50 yards and quite sudden. I need the flexibility of being able to adjust quickly to any number of angles, and a bipod does not allow that.

A luxury item for varmint hunting with a muzzleloader is a range finder. I have a Bushnell Yardage Pro that I use extensively. It serves two purposes. First, I take range readings from blinds so that I have a good idea of distance to specific points when a coyote comes in on a call or if I have set up a hog blind near a feeder or pond. There is normally no time to take such readings as a varmint comes in, but it is valuable as a method of discerning where I can confidently take a shot before I begin calling. Since I am not technically proficient enough to try a shot on a coyote-sized target beyond 150 yards, I find points that are within 100 yards. When a varmint crosses that imaginary line or gets close to it, I prepare to take my shot. Otherwise I keep on calling to lure him further in or wait until he comes in naturally. I also like a range finder because it tells me how much distance I have to close during a stalk before I can consider taking a shot. Distances on the open plains or in mesquite laced canyons can be deceiving and the range finder gives me an extra edge.

Another item that I like is a lightweight backpack, not so much for the standard muzzle-loading supplies that are in it but for all the other stuff: calls, extra clothing, snacks, range finder, binoculars, camera, and water bottles. It is easier to negotiate the backpack when moving in on a site than having a bunch of extra equipment hanging off my neck or stuck in my pants to slow my progress. During coyote and especially hog hunts in Texas I will often be out on my own for several hours. The backpack also makes a convenient rest for long-range set shots when I am not using a bipod. Make sure the pack has a dependable means of remaining closed or you could lose an expensive piece of support equipment.

Whether you're after reduced pelt damage for light game or excellent killing power for heavy, tough game, a muzzle-loading rifle can provide both. Modern muzzleloaders and properly configured loads can be accurate, dependable, quick to reload, and lethal. They won't rival conventional guns for multiple shots or extreme ranges but they can effectively provide economical and lethal service in a wide variety of hunting conditions. They can also be excellent support guns for special hunting circumstances where smokeless rounds are not as effective. All in all, I've found muzzleloaders to be credible performers on a wide variety of game.

Rabbits

The Plains have large populations of jackrabbits and cottontails. Shooting limits are liberal. Cottontails should not be handled during the warm months because of the slim chance that they might have tularemia, or "rabbit disease." Ticks and fleas usually carry the disease to rabbits. The sickness is contracted from handling infected animals. Infected animals will die within seven days of a hard freeze. It is then usually safe to handle cottontails. Because of the cottontail's preference for heavy cover, I normally use a shotgun for hunting. I have my best luck with a load of #5 or #6 shot over eighty or ninety grains of black powder. The black powder revolver is effective for rabbits in either .36 or .44 caliber. I thoroughly enjoy the .32 and .36 percussion rifle for rabbit hunting.

The jackrabbit is much larger than the cottontail and a completely different type of game. The jackrabbit is a hare, meaning that its young are born fully haired and open-eyed. Jackrabbits are born in the open and can travel within a day or so of birth. They are much more independent than the helpless little cottontail.

Jacks are most commonly hunted by walking them out of cover. It is surprising how little cover it takes to conceal a jack. When forced to, most jacks will invariably run fifty or so yards and then stop to look at what spooked them. That is when a hunter gets his best shot. Guns of .50 caliber or larger are hard on jackrabbits. Keep a .50 down loaded with around fifty grains of powder when hunting jacks or the ball will tear them to pieces. Head shots are preferable but somewhat unlikely at great range. I prefer a long-barrel, small-caliber rifle with fine sights for this type of shooting. Normally, I flush and roll them with a double-barrel muzzle-loading

Rabbit-Getter—The T/C New Englander shotgun was excellent for brush hunting of rabbits.

shotgun. Young jackrabbits are not bad eating, but older ones are tough, stringy, and gamey. I'd rather eat cottontails any day.

Squirrels

There are a number of substantial squirrel populations on the Plains, and hunting is not bad because they are not popular in most areas. Hedge apple trees were planted by the millions in shelter belts during the Dust Bowl of the 1930s. They are an excellent habitat for squirrels today. Trees are not very tall on the arid Plains, so shots are not long.

I prefer a muzzleloader shotgun for squirrel hunting, but a small-caliber rifle or even pistols or revolvers will do very nicely. Black powder revolvers are quite effective for taking squirrels because ranges can be short. Keep your loads low, as it does not take much to dispatch them.

Crows

During the fall, great numbers of ravens work their way across the Central Plains. Shooting can be monotonous because of their numbers. A light load of #7

Long-Range Varmint Shooting—Long-range shooting is difficult with an open sight muzzleloader. The odds are evened through patience, concealment, and planning.

½ shot and seventy grains of powder is an effective shotgun load. I normally position myself at the edge of a shelter belt and call them as they pass. Great shooting, but the bird itself is not worth eating.

The old-timers ate them and I've heard tell that they weren't considered "too bad." I'm not sure what that really means and I don't intend to find out.

Pioneer Tough

What is of special interest to those of us concerned with the history of the Plains is the fact that all of these animals, as well as the raccoon and opossum, were considered fair game and acceptable eating by the pioneers. Old-timers would eat almost anything to survive. It is easy for us to turn up our well-fed noses today at the idea of eating these animals. But animals, but when we consider just how tough it really was surviving those early years, I believe a person must develop an admiration for the strength of will and courage that these people must have had. We develop a better idea of the little things that modern historians tend to overlook. These tough, independent plainsmen made this country the settled land that it is today. Their guns were the tools of survival and absolutely essential if a man intended to exist in a hostile environment. The legacy of the rifle and shotgun is cherished today by people of the Plains. Without realizing why, many have maintained the important relationship between man and his guns from the lessons handed down from our pioneer ancestors.

14

Muzzle-Loading's Future

IN THE 21ST CENTURY, IT MAY BE DIFFICULT TO IMAGINE MUCH of a future for muzzle-loading weapons and historical arms. Some trends seem to point in the other direction. There is an element of the population that would like to end all hunting and shooting. Many urban citizens see guns of any type as little more than deadly threats to their peace and safety. The old argument over gun control is going to continue and I'm sure some compromises will be made.

I can imagine a situation when all hunting will be limited to primitive arms, but that is a worst-case scenario and probably won't take place. The wealth of a land can be demonstrated by the numbers of wildlife that survive within its boundaries. Wildlife in Africa and the southern hemisphere is under far greater pressure than in the wealthier nations because the richer nations can afford to spend the funds necessary for animal survival. The main point is that most of this money comes from the hunter through taxes on his equipment and land usage. Although many don't realize it, the achievements of our federal and state game management departments in preserving wildlife may go down as one of the great success stories of the 20th century. The land, where game took such a beating in the 19th century, may become the last refuge for all wildlife in the twenty-first.

Working the Forge— Bruce Kenyon demonstrates the use of a forge at a reenactment at Fort Larned, Kansas. Such demonstrations attract more visitors each year as modern Americans learn their heritage.

I am a very lucky man because I enjoy hunting and live in an area of tremendous hunting opportunities. I travel to Texas to hunt feral hogs and javelina in March. I hunt turkeys in the spring beginning in April. In the summer I can hunt prairie dogs and jackrabbits. In August there is dove hunting. Early muzzleloader deer season begins in September, American pronghorn in October, Colorado elk in the fall, and upland birds in November through January. I hunt deer in December and January, coyotes primarily in January through March, and then begin all over again. I hunt at least forty-five weekends out of the year. It is my way of getting out of the office and away from the Internet and telephone. If I were limited to muzzleloader-only guns, I could do it all with a primitive .50 caliber sidelock and double-barrel 12 gauge shotgun. I know that because I have done it. I have also hunted in Africa with a muzzleloader and did not feel handicapped. In fact, it was exhilarating to enjoy the challenge of black powder hunting on the other side of the Atlantic.

Sidelock and In-Line Muzzleloaders

Muzzleloaders today are of primitive and modern design. Modern in-line rifles and shotguns have become popular because of special seasons established by the states. I use and enjoy both sidelock and modern in-line rifles and shotguns. I do not believe that the advantage of modern in-line is as great as many claim, but they are effective and can be more convenient than sidelocks.

For a while there was a great proliferation of in-line companies and designs on the market with so many annual product introductions that it was difficult to document all of them. During that period the historical replicas sold in steady but uninspiring numbers. Fully eighty percent of the new gun market today is in the in-line market. The majority of the small in-line companies have passed on. They were unable to compete with the tremendous marketing expenditures nor could they afford to radically update models each year to keep up with the large in-line companies.

A technology race developed among the inline companies that promised improved ignition, higher velocities, greater range, less cleaning, radical new gun concepts, polymer stocks, closed ignition systems, camouflage finishes, fiber-optic sights, and innumerable other gadgets and gismos. It was evident that the ultimate goal was to produce a muzzleloader that looked and performed exactly like a modern cartridge rifle. I rode that bandwagon for a while in hunting articles and gun reviews until I realized that the trend was eventually going to be self-defeating and could endanger the future of special muzzleloader-only seasons.

Extravagant ballistic claims have backfired on the in-line companies. States are moving toward primitive muzzleloader seasons and designing regulations that exclude many modern in-lines that use pellet propellants, smokeless powder, 209 primer ignition, sabot projectiles, scopes, and closed ignition systems. I believe this trend will continue. Muzzleloader-only seasons were originally idealized as primitive arms seasons and in-line trends have undermined that special status. The more radical new in-line designs become and the more extravagant the claims, the more likely that they will be excluded from primitive firearms only seasons.

As population growth continues and urban areas progressively intrude on our wildlife areas, there has been a trend toward regulating big game hunting to slug gun and muzzleloader-only hunting. While some recent research indicates that shooting accidents are not affected by going this route, the public perception that short-range guns are safer remains. Primitive sidelock muzzleloaders fit right into this nitch. They are more accurate than many slug guns, are very effective hunting tools, and do not intimidate many urban residents. The primitive rifle market is not going to disintegrate. My advice is that a person who plans on owning only one muzzleloader should seriously consider a sidelock before an in-line. No matter where you hunt in the United States, an open sight sidelock round ball gun will fit into the local muzzleloader hunting regulations. If the time should come when you want to engage in historical celebrations or primitive shoots, your sidelock will probably be accepted. An in-line will not be.

A Need for Active Involvement

Achievements in the management of deer and turkey populations make up another great success story. Waterfowl abound because of public and private habitat establishment. All of these gains come from game management and not from an end to regulated hunting. It was hunter involvement that helped save much of the wildlife and it will be the same forces that preserve wildlife in the future. If you want to do your part in saving wildlife, buy a hunting license, even if you don't hunt. This statement may sound like a contradiction but in the United States today it is a cold, hard fact. Africa's debacle in many countries has taught us that when wildlife has no economic value to the people, the wildlife is destroyed.

Most of those who engage in primitive black powder hunting today are more experienced. The muzzleloader hunter is usually a person who has developed skills to the point that black powder presents more of a challenge than modern rifles and shotguns. It seems that the share of the population that actively hunts will continue to decrease in the face of urban development. This will leave more of a hardcore central group of hunters who will battle to preserve the sport and environment. The trend now is toward less hunters who are involved in many hunting activities.

In order to be successful in the face of some vocal opposition, muzzleloaders will have to align themselves with all hunting interests. When various gun control laws are put forward, it is easy for the muzzle-loading hunter to sit back and believe that since it has nothing to do with black powder, it really doesn't matter because it doesn't affect his interests. The challenge is more involved than just individual interests. If legislation can achieve a ban on automatic weapons today, how long will it be before primitive gun interests find themselves in a similar battle and with weaker numbers? If hunting is banned in California or New England, how long before the lightly populated Plains are under a similar assault? The fewer of us there are, the more we will need to watch out for each other's interests.

This position doesn't mean that all of us need to agree on the value of or the need for semiautomatic military rifles for hunting, but it does mean that we need to closely evaluate all new regulations and proposals for legislation and be vocal in our opposition when we perceive that any of them are even remotely threatening to our own interests. When we attack each other, we destroy all. Primitive muzzleloader interests that attack in-line interests; in-line interests that sue states to further their profits in the name of hunter equality; hunting writers who attack semiautomatic rifles as "terrorist rifles"; and those who demand that they have special privileges at the expense of others are all examples of short-sighted ignorance. The opposition will use every opportunity to divide and conquer.

Who and what will suffer in the long run? Wildlife, for one, will suffer. All hunting interests, for another. Everyone will be the loser in the long run. United we will stand, divided we are conquered. Wildlife with no value and perceived as a nuisance will be destroyed by the march of urban development. I almost wrote "civilization" instead of "urban development," but a truly civilized community looks upon all aspects of the challenge and is not swayed by the propaganda or special interests of a few, especially if it is not scientifically based. Those who would end all hunting use nonscientific sources and flagrantly ignore the lessons of recent history in third-world nations and the United States of the 19th and early 20th centuries.

A Bright Future for Living History

It might appear that living history reenactment will remain a hobby for a very small percentage of the population. I am inclined to disagree. Spectator numbers will grow as our youth become more and more oblivious to our written history. Living history and the fascination for old-times and old ways will continue to draw the curious in greater numbers as our civilization becomes more complex.

Wild & Wooly West—Members of a popular reenactment troop, Wild & Wooly West, perform at Dodge City's Boot Hill Museum. Presentations of this type are popular and entertaining.

Right now it is often difficult for historical sites to maintain themselves because of limited involvement, but the pendulum will swing back. The important thing is to maintain the resources of today for the future. Communities can be short-sighted in this area and it is up to historical groups to do what they can to maintain and promote historical sites.

For many, it will only be a matter of time until the urge to try a role will take precedence. Many will investigate their own area and local history in order to re-create and appreciate that community. I don't do Revolutionary War, Native American, or longhunter reenactment because I am so busy with Santa Fe Trail and Old West history, but I am always drawn to living history events in other areas when I am there. I have great appreciation for those presentations because I know the work and research involved in preparing and presenting them.

The Plains

One of the goals of this book is to create an interest in the history and natural beauty of the Plains region of North America. For too long, the Plains have been

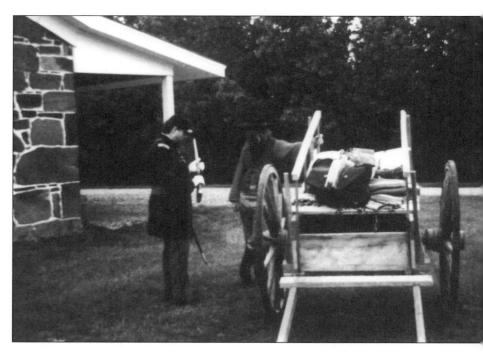

Green River Wagon—Old-time equipment such as this Green River Wagon at Fort Larned National Historic Site is very popular with reenactment audiences. Such items also put visitors in touch with the back-breaking labor that frontiersmen endured.

viewed as just a dull, featureless landscape that separates the scenic mountains of the Far West from the forests of the East. The Plains is every bit as beautiful and unique as the others. Once a person develops an understanding and appreciation of the Plains environment, a new way of looking at the Plains will develop. Only Africa provides more varied opportunities for the broad range of hunting and fishing that exist on the prairies and plains of North America. It is a rich treasure that many have overlooked. There is so much more to the world than piles of rocks and shade trees. The Plains environment presents a grand part of it.

As for the black powder plainsman, I see his numbers increasing. The legacy of the plainsman is just as interesting and challenging as the mountain man or the longhunter. He just came along a little bit later in history.

15

Capsule Chronology: 1820–1876

WHILE SITTING AROUND THE CAMPFIRE, IT IS NOT UNUSUAL FOR buckskinners and reenactors to become involved in debates concerning historical dates and events on the Great Plains. The following list is a short chronology of events that occurred during the era of concern for this book. While this list will certainly not stop the debates concerning when events took place, it may help focus them.

1820–1829

1820
- Major Stephen H. Long led an expedition up the Platte to the Rocky Mountains in an attempt to locate the sources of the Red and Arkansas rivers.
- Daniel Boone died on the family homestead in Missouri.
- The Missouri Compromise was adopted, admitting Missouri as a slave state and Maine as a free state.

1821
- Mexico, now independent of Spain, released American traders from prison for trading violations.
- William Becknell made the journey that established the Santa Fe Trail. Yes, there was another expedition. John McKnight and Thomas James were the leaders.

- Hugh Glenn and Jacob Fowler led an expedition to New Mexico to trap.
- Stephen Austin began scouting out lands in Texas for a colony at his father's request.

1822

- William Ashley and Andrew Henry formed the Rocky Mountain Fur Company.
- William Becknell used wagons and the Cimarron Cutoff to establish a quicker route to Santa Fe. Benjamin Cooper also tried the route and almost failed crossing the *Jornada del Muerto*.

1823

- Robert and John McKnight began trading for horses with the Comanches.

1824

- William Ashley began following the Platte River route to the Rocky Mountains.
- Traders began forming caravans to Santa Fe for protection against Indian raids. The caravans would usually break up within 100 miles of Santa Fe.

1828

- Several caravans were attacked by Indians along the Santa Fe Trail.

1829

- Major Bennet Riley was assigned to escort a caravan to Santa Fe as far as the Mexican border. Oxen were used to prove their value as draft animals.

1830–1839
1831

- Hall J. Kelley formed a society to promote settlement of the Oregon territory.

1832

- Nathaniel Wyeth crossed the Plains in an effort to start a settlement in Oregon.
- Jedediah Smith was killed while crossing the *Jornada del Muerto* of the Santa Fe Trail.
- Captain Benjamin Bonneville entered the fur trade and established a wagon route over South Pass.
- The steamboat *Yellowstone* reached Fort Union of the Missouri River.

1833

- William and Charles Bent and Ceran St.Vrain built Bent's Old Fort at the head of the northwest loop of the Arkansas River route of the Santa Fe Trail.

1834

- Colonel Henry Dodge led an expedition into the Southwest to meet with the Comanches and Wichitas.
- Bill Sublette and Robert Campbell built Fort William near the mouth of the Laramie River.

1835

- Colonel Dodge made another trip through the southern plains to meet with Indians.

1836

- Texas declared and won independence from Mexico.

1837

- A smallpox epidemic on the Upper Missouri took a staggering toll of Indians.

1839

- The Mormons moved from Missouri to Nauvoo, Illinois.
- John Charles Fremont and Joseph Nicollet explored the eastern portion of the northern Great Plains.

1840–1849

1841

- The Bidwell-Bartleson party crossed the Plains on the first emigrant train to California and Oregon.
- The Republic of Texas attempted and failed to open commerce with Santa Fe.

1842

- Lansford Hastings crossed the Plains with a group of emigrants. He later became the author of *The Emigrants' Guide to Oregon and California*.
- John Charles Fremont led an expedition from Missouri to South Pass. His guide was Kit Carson.

1843

- Fremont attempted another expedition over the Oregon Trail and parts of the West Coast.

- John Deere began manufacture of his plow, an invention that would revolution-ize agriculture on the plains.

1844

- Joseph Smith, leader of the Mormons, was murdered in Carthage, Illinois. Brigham Young assumed leadership and a need to relocate the church away from civilization was established.
- First observations of the sudden decline of the buffalo on the Plains were made.

1845

- Lieutenant J. W. Abert explored northeastern New Mexico and northwestern Texas.
- Colonel Stephen Watts Kearny led the First Dragoons to South Pass and returned to Missouri.
- The annexation of Texas was approved.

1846

- President James Knox Polk ordered General Zachary Taylor to the Rio Grande in an effort to provoke the Mexicans.
- War with Mexico was declared.
- Stephen Kearny's Army of the West marched across the Plains to Bent's Old Fort.

1847

- Brigham Young led Mormon pioneers westward across the plains and estab-lished settlements near the Great Salt Lake.

1848

- Mexico ceded most of the Southwest and California to the United States, end-ing the war. The Rio Grande became the official border.
- Gold was discovered in California near Sutter's Mill.
- Mormons began moving in large numbers to the Great Salt Lake.
- Fort Kearny was built on the Platte River to protect the Oregon–California Trail.

1849

- The Gold Rush began, flooding the Oregon–California Trail.
- Captain Randolph B. Marcy blazed an emigrant trail from Fort Smith, Arkansas, to Santa Fe.

1850–1859

1850

- Fort Atkinson was established near present-day Dodge City, Kansas, to protect a new mail route from across the Plains to Santa Fe. Mail to Salt Lake City was also established.

1851

- The Fort Laramie Treaty was signed with several Plains tribes to protect the Oregon-California Trail.

1852

- Randolph Marcy explored the sources of the Red River.

1853

- The Fort Atkinson Treaty was signed with Comanches, Kiowas, and Kiowa-Apaches to try to settle the issue of the Santa Fe Trail.

1854

- Russell, Majors and Waddell, one of the largest of the freight-hauling companies, was established to meet a contract to supply new army posts on the Plains.
- A trading post near present-day Pueblo, Colorado, was destroyed by the Indians. The Plains Indian war was greatly aggravated.

1855

- General William S. Harney led an expedition that followed the Arkansas River and then went north into western Nebraska in an effort to punish the Sioux and several other Plains tribes.

1856

- Harney restored relations with the Sioux.
- The Mormons began a series of migrations to Salt Lake City using handcarts rather than wagons. Dozens died of exposure and starvation.

1858

- The first transcontinental stagecoach routes were established from Missouri to California.
- Green Russell established Denver, Colorado, and a second Gold Rush. The Smokey Hill Trail was established as a result.

1859

- William Bent was appointed Indian Agent for the Kiowas and Comanches. He urged the establishment of forts near Bent's New Fort and along the Pawnee Fork in central Kansas.
- Colonel Edwin O. Sumner established Camp on Pawnee Fork.

1860–1869

1860

- The Pony Express commenced operations.
- Major John Sedgwick and Captain Samuel D. Sturgis waged campaigns against the Comanches and Kiowas. Fort Larned was established to replace Fort Atkinson and Camp Alert (Camp on Pawnee Fork).

1861

- The Civil War began.
- The transcontinental telegraph line was completed.
- The Pony Express failed.
- Confederate soldiers tried but failed to capture New Mexico. Kit Carson was a commander for Union forces.

1862

- The Homestead Act was passed and provided free land for settlers.

1863

- Colonel Henry Sibley and General Alfred Sully campaigned against the Sioux in North Dakota.

1864

- Fort Larned was raided by Indians. The Indians stole 172 animals.
- Fort Zarah was established 40 miles east of Fort Larned.
- An escort system was established between Fort Larned and Fort Lyon, New Mexico, to protect trade caravans to Santa Fe.

1865

- The Civil War ended.
- General Patrick Connor led an expedition against the Indians in the Powder River country.

1866
- General Granville Dodge became the chief engineer of the Union Pacific. Construction of the Transcontinental Railroad began.
- Captain Henry Fetterman's command was massacred at Fort Phil Kearny.

1867
- General Winfield S. Hancock launched a foolish expedition against the Cheyenne along the Arkansas River out of Fort Larned. He managed to burn one empty Indian village.
- The Wagon Box Fight took place near Fort Phil Kearny.
- John McCoy established cattle shipments by railroad from Abilene, Kansas.

1868
- Fort Phil Kearny was abandoned.
- The Cheyennes, Comanches, and Kiowas rose up along the Santa Fe Trail.
- Colonel George A. Forsyth fought the Battle of Beecher's Island against Roman Nose near Fort Wise, Colorado.

1869
- General George A. Custer launched a winter campaign against the Cheyennes and Arapahoes.
- The Transcontinental Railroad was completed.

1870–1879
1871
- Ellsworth, Kansas, became a center for shipping cattle by railroad to the East.

1872
- Dodge City was established to ship cattle on the Atchison, Topeka, and Santa Fe Railroad and to take advantage of the buffalo hide trade.
- Wichita, Kansas, began shipping operations of cattle by railroad.
- Yellowstone National Park was established.

1873
- Congress passed the Timber Culture Act, which allowed homesteaders to own a second 160-acre homestead by establishing a timber claim. By planting trees, a homesteader could double his Homestead Act claim.
- Joseph Glidden invented barbed wire.
- Seven million cattle were shipped out of Kansas. The price of cattle collapsed and a financial panic in the cattle trade took place.

1874

- The Battle of Adobe Walls was fought between buffalo hunters and a Cheyenne–Arapahoe alliance.
- Colonel Randald Mackenzie defeated the Cheyennes in Palo Duro Canyon, Texas.
- The Great Southern Buffalo Herd was destroyed by commercial hunters with the blessing of the United States government.
- Custer entered the Black Hills in response to a gold rush.

1875

- Charles Goodnight and John Adair established the JA Ranch along the Palo Duro.

1876

- Custer and five companies of the 7th Cavalry were massacred at the Battle of the Little Big Horn on June 25.
- James Butler (Wild Bill) Hickok was murdered by Jack McCall in Deadwood, Dakota Territory, on August 2, over one month after the Custer massacre.

16

Creating the Historical
Dramatic Monologue

DRAMATIC MONOLOGUES ARE BECOMING INCREASINGLY POPU-
lar at celebrations, rendezvous, and historic site activities. One interesting trend
involves "grave conversations" activities at historical cemetery sites. Audiences love
them and they add greatly to celebration activities. There is an appeal in these dramatic monologues not only to the audience but also to the performers.

The historical dramatic monologue represents the greatest of the reenactment
challenges because it calls for more than just knowledge or craftsmanship. The dramatic monologue demands that a reenactor entertain and inform his audience
through the performance of a historical character by a staged drama or rhetorical
reading. Presenting dramatic monologues can be satisfying because the presenter
is in charge of the presentation and can control the content and order. The more
deeply involved one becomes in living history reenactment, the greater the assump-
tion of increased levels of knowledge. It is often difficult to find a format where
that mastery can be shared with the audience. Observers of on-site craftsmanship
or location reenactments are often not able to ask more than the fundamental
questions of what, where, or why, or they are reluctant to engage a reenactor with
complex, in-depth inquiries.

A dramatic monologue can also be frustrating because, like any dramatic presentation, the rewards can be great but the chances of failure are great as well. The
ultimate goal of a historical dramatic monologue is for the reenactor to not only
share historical knowledge but also create an emotional bond between the audi-

Print Olive—The author performing notorious rancher I. P. "Print" Olive at the 2006 AFOWR national finals in Wichita, Kansas.

ence and the historical character. The audience is given an opportunity to experience a connection with the "real" person as well as gain a superficial knowledge of how things looked, were done, and why. Organization of such a presentation is complex because, in actuality, the reenactor is creating a short story told from that character's perspective that must entertain as well as inform.

There are three general styles of historical dramatic monologues. One is to assume the role of a real person. This is the most common method used by professional actors. Besides excellent professional performances like Henry Fonda's Clarence Darrow, James Whitmore's Harry Truman, or Van Ann Moore's Libby Custer, I have seen credible performances of Susan Mogaffin, William Bent, and Brigham Young by talented amateurs. A second type of monologue is to create a composite fictional character whose monologue represents the typical views and experiences of a historical character in the same circumstances. I like to do this style of reenactment because I have the freedom to place my characters in historical situations to give an outline of historical circumstances (notorious Texas rancher I. P. "Print" Olive, professional bison hunter Jonah William Campbell, or Santa Fe Trail trader John Walker, for example). However, doing such a reenactment must also be reflective of real-life situations and not an episodic dramatic adventure into the world of make-believe (such as the preposterous "Little Big Man") to maintain credibility. A popular third method is a journal reading of a real character (such as a member of the Donner Party, a Civil War soldier, or a woman's diary). The third, the easiest for a beginner, requires the least dramatic skills and can be very compelling, especially if it is well written and dramatically edited for the monologue.

So, how does one go about creating a historical dramatic character and monologue? First of all, it is necessary to decide which type of presentation you would be most comfortable presenting and your goals for the presentation. Are you actor enough to carry such a performance? Would it be easier for you to dress in costume and simply read from a journal? Do you want to:

- Inform your audience about a specific historical character?
- Create a portrait or snapshot of a historical situation, organization, or occupation?
- Relate the events of a single event or series of historical incidents?
- Recreate as much as possible an ambiance or feel for a historical location?
- Demonstrate a craft or skill that was critical to that time period?

With some characterizations you may want to accomplish all of those goals, but you need to remember some critical rules of dramatic or public speaking presentations.

Your presentation must have a beginning, middle, and ending in a logical, understandable sequence for the audience to follow. Most dramatic presentations build toward a climax or high point of action that moves or stirs the audience. You should aim your presentation toward an audience with general rather than specific knowledge and must include the fundamentals of who, what, when, where, and why.

You must gauge your audience so as not to offend or displease with your presentation. I would never consider doing an Indian for a group of Native Americans, for instance, or tell a horrific story of Donner Party cannibalism or read the Texas Comanche atrocity diaries to a group of young children. In the first case, unless I was extremely knowledgeable, I risk cultural offensiveness. In the second, there are better times and older audiences for appreciation of such stories.

Twenty minutes is a reasonable time to plan to hold a general audience and, unless you are an exceptional speaker or performer, you should not expect to hold their attention much longer than that. If your presentation is one of several, fifteen

Sarah Fleming— Debbie Edens performing Sara Edens. Notice the use of props and careful staging for her presentation.

minutes is adequate. If your performance is interesting to them, thirty minutes is enough. An hour will not make it better.

So, if you only have twenty to thirty minutes to make a presentation, how do you inform an audience of historical points or specific happenings without misleading or boring them? This is where the concept of an historical snapshot becomes so important to a dramatic monologue. Chances are that you can ramble on for hours about your time period, trade, or character. You've made the study and have the interest. But in order to relate to a general audience, you can only include bits and pieces of the total picture and hope that you have accomplished your goals. It is for that reason this I like to do the location-specific semi-fictional style of reenactment.

For instance, if I am in Dodge City doing my buffalo hunting character of 1874, I will give a logical excuse for why I am there. If I am at Fort Larned and doing my Santa Fe trader character in 1868, I tell what I am doing and why I am there. I can interchange those characters for both locations. However, if I am in Bent's Old Fort and doing my Santa Fe trader or buffalo hunter, my story changes considerably. Bent's Old Fort didn't exist in 1868 or 1874. I must either take the same character and move him back twenty-five years or change my character completely. Chances are I can do this for these types of fictional characterizations. I can never make gunman Wild Bill Hickok or rancher Print Olive work for Bent's Old Fort any more than for Valley Forge or Gettysburg because such characterizations simply do not work for the time period or location.

I can create another buffalo hunter or Santa Fe trader for the Bent's Old Fort time period, change my dress to the appropriate date, and present much of the same information. I must remember two critical elements, however. Firstly, I only know what I would have known up to that specific time period, and secondly, my content must reflect the thinking of that time period.

It is for this reason that I like to create a reference guide for each portrayal, whether he is fictional or real, before I ever begin writing or planning a monologue. In that reference guide I list the important happenings in that character's life by date and include all historical elements that I believe would have interested the person and will have some appeal to the audience.

In my John Walker, the Santa Fe Trail trader, I want to present my audience with an overview of trader life on the Santa Fe Trail. Therefore I begin his experiences with the Trail and end it at the time period and location that I am portraying, usually central Kansas in 1868. I could do the same 1868 character in Council Grove, Fort Dodge, Fort Union, Santa Fe, or any other trail location and present essentially the same information. At 58 years of age, it is credible for me to portray a man of age 60 in 1868. It is not so easy to portray a man in his thirties at Bent's Old Fort in 1843, but I could as long as my equipment and knowledge ends between 1843 and 1849. With this character, however, my presentation would be much more interesting later in life and I would probably change him to better fit the Bent's Old Fort era.

I do not tell about John Walker. I do John Walker telling about his world, a subtle and most important perspective. I like to do my presentations as if each member of the audience has just run into my character at the location where I am presenting the monologue. For instance, if I am John Walker at Fort Larned in the spring of 1868, I am most concerned with what has happened to me recently. My character is waiting for a military escort for his caravan because of Indian uprisings along the Santa Fe Trail. My character lost his only son to Indians in the area the year before so I am bitter, still in a state of mourning, and looking forward to retirement. I am also concerned about the condition of my wagons, goods, livestock, and men. I talk about those things frequently and allow the audience to filter out the rest. I can go back and tell an unusual story in my personal history, such as William Becknell's return to Franklin, Missouri, when I was a youngster in 1822; or my relationship with William Waldo on the trail in the early years of the trade; or my sadness at the loss of good friend Charles Bent in the 1848 Taos Rebellion; or Civil War encounters at the Star Fort at Fort Union in 1862. I can tell these stories about real characters and locations that I have researched and present a capsule view of Santa Fe Trail history for the audience. My character is simply a vehicle to present the ambiance of Santa Fe Trail history.

When I work up my character, whether fictional or real, I concern myself with his persona. I want to know his religion, his family history, his politics, his values,

Wyatt Earp—Many reenactors do not have formal presentations but choose to play their role individually to people they meet at historical events. These one-on-one meetings where the reenactor stays in character greatly add to any event.

his great loves and disappointments, his prejudices, and his way of dealing with life. I want to reflect all of these elements in my mannerisms and offhand remarks, even if I do not specifically present them to the audience. It is for this reason that I do not portray Indians, choosing to portray myself as if I lived in that time period, that is, as a white Anglo Saxon Protestant of a working class family. My characters generally reflect those qualities because I have most of my study and insight based on such family and political history. I do not want to portray what I am, a baby boomer born in the late 1940s. I want to reflect the mores, beliefs, and attitudes of a man of an earlier time period as honestly as possible without reflecting my own present-day beliefs. The last thing I want to do is reflect modern day political agendas, a common mistake made by many amateur and professional reenactors. I know of no better way of acquiring such insight than by reading personal journals, speeches, and writings of the period. I may read a history book or article summarizing a character or situation of a specific time, but I want to read personal journals to see how people really thought back then. Generally, these historical characters were not environmentalists, libertarians, Native American apologists, women's libbers, or pro-choice advocates. Compared to our day, they were more superstitious, racist, and ethnocentric, and less scientifically and far more philosophically oriented. They weren't bad people but rather men and women of their time, reflecting the experiences and teachings of their lives rather than ours. If the audience is uncomfortable without being downright offended with some opinions or statements, then so much the better. It helps them evaluate and compare the modern world and their own character. It can increase insight into the person and the times. A presentation walks a fine line here, however, and careful evaluation of what the performance can gain or lose needs to made before inclusion of certain shocking or outrageous statements.

Inclusion or rejection of material becomes an important part of dramatic monologues. For instance, I have spent quite a lot of time and resources investigating Kit Carson, although I have never done a monologue about him because I don't believe I am physically right for the portrayal. One of the unusual claims made about Carson is that he fathered a number of illegitimate Indian children. Some tribal members recall their Carson ancestry with pride. The fact might be an enlightening piece of information for the audience. It could also be construed into a form of character assassination by anti-Carson factions, especially those who are critical of his treatment of the Indian.

I have no written documentation of these children and Carson does not mention them in any of his statements. I would mention his brief second marriage to Making-Our-Road and his Indian daughter by his first marriage because they are clearly documented. I believe that the illegitimacy issue is material that might be included in an Indian reenactment, which would naturally be based more upon oral rather than written history. My goal is to provide as accurate a picture as possible of Carson, his life, his times, and his place in history. I have to evaluate how such material aids in that goal and how it competes with other material. I believe the material is too historically questionable for my goals and I would not include it in my monologue.

This is the point at which dramatic monologues become the ultimate challenge of the reenactor and historian. We move beyond knowledge of time, events, science, and location into the philosophical and emotional world of all men and women. We take our study to the human level where we strive to learn what makes people tick and mirror it for our audience as part of our depiction of a character profile. That is the point where learning begins and living history comes to life, not only for the audience but also for the reenactor.

17

Old West Reenactors—Re-creating the Old West with Style and Accuracy

DARK-CLAD, ARMED MEN ADVANCE IN A LINE DOWN THE FRONtier town's dusty streets. Waiting to face them is a homesteader and his family determined to stand for their rights and defend them with their guns. Harsh words and threats are spoken as the gunmen attempt to impose their will. Moments later guns flash and men fall on both sides. The gunmen are dead and women rush to the wounded homesteader. Amid tears of grief the women hear the last words of their husband and father. He has stood for his beliefs but at the cost of his life. The melodrama ends with the lesson that violence in the Old West was necessary at times, but usually at a terrible price.

The players assemble and bow to the applause of the crowd. Moments later, as the actors gather their props to make way for the next melodrama, Wild Bill Hickok steps forward to tell of his life and accomplishments. Still later the crowd is entertained by a reenactment of Frank Butler and Annie Oakley's Buffalo Bill's Wild West act. And so it goes through the day as one presentation after another assembles before the audience and a panel of judges during a tournament day for the Reenactment Guild of America.

The American Federation of Old West Reenactors was formed in 1998 with the lofty goal of becoming the premier sanctioning body of group and individual reenactors. It was a national nonprofit organization open exclusively to theatrical arts groups and individual performers who are committed to the highest standards of historical accuracy and period dress. In its short lifetime the group made significant inroads toward accomplishing its charter and claimed a membership

Annie Oakley and Frank Butler— This Annie Oakley and Frank Butler presentation recreates one of Annie's famous acts for Buffalo Bill's Wild West show. Specialty acts such as this are popular for many community celebrations.

of over 400. The organization was replaced by the short-lived American Federation of Old West Reenactors in 2005 and evolved into the Reenactment Guild of America (RGA) in 2007. This group is composed of both professional and amateur reenactors who perform regularly in motion pictures, on the stage, and at historical pageants and celebrations.

For those who are infatuated with the history of the Old West, an interest in reliving and performing the past can become an enjoyable diversion. Throughout this country there are a number of individuals and groups striving to re-create historical characters. Reenactors gather to re-create Civil War battles, Indian Wars engagements, military, mountain man, cowboy, outlaw, and lawman historical gatherings. Living history demonstrations by dedicated amateurs and professionals grace historical pagents, historic sites, and celebrations throughout the country. Living history reenactors often do dramatic monologues for the purpose of educating and entertaining audiences on special characters, trades, or lifestyles of the Old West. These people become experts on the lives and lifestyles of such well-known characters as Buffalo Bill Cody, Wild Bill Hickok, Wyatt Earp, William Bonney, George Armstrong Custer, Sitting Bull, Belle Starr, or Annie Oakley. Others will choose more obscure characters for study and presentation. Still others will concentrate on primitive crafts and skills for demonstration without a special character in mind. Many historical sites will have groups that entertain the public with dramatic or comedic sketches of local characters. The challenge and enjoyment of living history presentations attract people from all walks of life and levels of education.

As someone who has been active in and a student of the art of reenactment for years, I have been encouraged by the growth of the activity and disturbed by the abuse of some representing themselves as historical characters. Some historical locations, especially national historic sites, have stringent rules regulating who can and

Comedy—Not all presentations are dramatic. Reenactment group Wild & Wooly West of Seymour, Texas, is known for its comedy sketches.

cannot act as a reenactor. Other locations seem willing to let anyone show up and represent him or herself as a historical character without questioning authenticity. For people who have spent significant time and resources investigating and re-creating historical figures for living history events, it is something of an insult to watch the uniformed represent themselves as historical characters. Watching so-called 19th century reenactors wearing penny loafers, Wrangler jeans, Resistol straw hats, snap button western shirts, Hollywood buscadero holster rigs, and wristwatches grates on the nerves of dedicated historical interpreters to say the least.

Modern reenactment guilds were created to address such problems for those interested in post–Civil War Old West history, circa 1865–1894. The RGA offers member benefits of sanctioned local and national competitions, copyright registry of group and individual member skits and plays, registration and recognition by casting agencies and film commissions, acting and stunt workshops, liability insurance, and a number of other enhancements to those who will strive to meet the standards and qualifications. The RGA Code of Ethics includes a pledge to faithfully remain 100 percent historically accurate to the clothing of the portrayed time period as well as to cultivate the highest standards of the performing arts. The overall goal is to provide development of the art to the highest professional level, with logistical and interpretive support to raise the Old West era to a level of national recognition and respectability that it deserves.

Three categories of performance are presently included in local, regional, and national competitions. The reenactment division involves historical skits, the living history division involves informal historical demonstrations, and the specialty act division involves historical dramatic monologues and special thematic presentations. Good acting skills as well as historical accuracy are a primary concern in member presentations.

Competing groups are judged in four categories: clothing, acting, stunts, and storyline. Teams perform twice at most events and performances are either in the form of a skit or a historical account. Each team has a time limit of five to fifteen minutes, and most of the dramatic presentations attempt to re-create actual historical events or circumstances. Topics may include the relationship between Doc Holiday and Wyatt Earp, Annie Oakley's introduction to Buffalo Bill Cody, opposition to carpetbagger injustices in post–Civil War Texas, or a good old-fashioned poker game shootout. The key to the competition is overall point accumulation. Awards are given for best actor/actress, best group performance, best costume, best stunt, and several other categories.

Those who have been involved in reenactment for a number of years will appreciate some genuinely positive potential for such an organization. A genuine impartial sanctioning body for historical reenactment can establish a benchmark of excellence for many local reenactment, and historical pageant groups to strive

Meade Gathering—Reenactment members, judges, and celebrities gather for a group photo. Notice the wide range of costumes and characters represented at such a function.

for it as part of their goals and objectives. Although the motion picture industry is naturally glamorized as part of the organization's scope of interest, the largest membership and greatest potential of such a sanctioning body involves improving and standardizing local pageants and historical sites. Too many reenactments and pageants are woefully short on historical and clothing accuracy and are not in the best interest of preserving this country's most important and influential national legend. The value of such a sanctioning body as a potential standard of excellence and means of referral for local communities wanting to find qualified resource personnel is exciting.

The common response to a survey of members was that each joined not only to learn from their fellow reenactors but to compete on a professional level with them. It is important to them that others with similar interests recognize their skill and research. Peer criticism is an important method of reinforcing and refining their performances.

18

Old West Reenactment Skits, Gunfights, and Plays

GUNFIGHTER PERFORMANCES ARE AMONG THE MOST POPULAR Old West reenactments. Performing a historically accurate drama with an Old West theme is a popular event for competitions, historical pageants, community celebrations, and historic site theme days. Gunfight skits are especially popular, but there are other occasions when historical dramas are well received. Normally, such presentations are outdoor affairs with all the accompanying headaches that go along with any activity that must deal with weather extremes. Usually there is a mix of amateur and professional actors involved in these presentations and stages are often based on whatever local facilities are available.

There are also competitions where various reenactment groups vie for trophies and prizes. Groups ranging in size from three to thirty can compete. Presentations can be comedies, dramas, and historical reenactments of actual events. The success of any presentation depends on a number of elements.

The Reenactment Guild of America is an organization of living historians, educators, entertainers, and reenactors dedicated to the preservation and education of the history of America's 19th century, primarily but not restricted to the American Old West. It is, as of this writing, the most current organization of this type.

Reenactment as Drama

Basic theater skills come into play for any presentation to be valuable. The audience is being told an entertaining and enlightening story. Special care should be taken to ensure that the presentation has a clear beginning, middle, and end. All

Playing Cowboy—
One of the author's first and favorite gunfight roles was as a vengeful rancher looking to "set things a-right!" Getting to handle a vintage Spencer carbine for the role didn't hurt. No matter what your age, playing cowboy is just plain fun.

theatrical presentations should build to a climax (the high point of action), which is normally at or near the end of the presentation. If that climatic event is a gunfight or showdown, there should be a logical reason for the showdown presented.

Some groups can produce a presentation with a loosely organized script. Others prefer a very tight script with exact phrases and movements clearly spelled out. If a troop of actors is experienced and familiar with each other, a loosely organized presentation will work very well. If a group is new and there are several amateur members in the acting troop, a tight script with exact movements is more comforting for the actors and will produce the most success.

The Reenactment Guild of America is dedicated to the accurate and historical presentation of life in the American West during the 19th century. Their Code of Ethics describes the basic goals of the organization:

It is the desire of the guild membership to preserve this part of American history and to provide a safe venue where the public may be both educated and entertained at the same time. All members of the guild will be expected to conduct themselves in a manner that will not bring discredit to RGA. RGA does not tolerate nor will it condone or support discrimination of any person or entity in any form or manner. RGA members will be expected to follow all the guild rules and guidelines set forth by the board and to adhere to all Local, State and Federal laws of the United States of America. Because historical truths are sometimes found to be fluid and open to interpretation, every effort will be made to insure that members portray their characters or events in a historically correct manner which shall include but is not restricted to clothing, utensils, weapons, behavior and speech. Questions regarding these areas will be professionally presented for clarification. Members, in response to such questions, will refrain from action or speech that could be construed as hostile. In all cases of competition, the judges will have final say on issues of safety or historical correctness.

No discourse will be allowed in front of the judges table. Performers must honor historical records and knowledge and should document such sources used in their presentations so that they may withstand critical review. RGA members will strive to assist each other in the pursuit of historical accuracy and understanding. Further, members will respect the integrity of historical records while investigating and interpreting the past during presentations as a matter of practice. Membership will also respect the presentations and portrayals of the past by all other members and will not resort to plagiarism. RGA members are to consider themselves as mentors/teachers to young and old alike and behave at all times while representing RGA in a manner above reproach. Inappropriate actions or behavior by any member is subject to review by the board and may result in expulsion of the member.

The Performers are professionals bound by a love of the Western frontier as well as a love for history and their fellow human being. These are values shared by all members of the guild.

RGA Judges' Instructions

The following are performance items that Reenactment Guild of America judges are instructed to evaluate. These same elements are critical for any historical drama:

- **Storyline:** The Show must have a beginning, middle, and ending! Introduce characters to the audience and develop characters as the story goes on. Plot must build to an adequate climax. You must have a story that comes to a proper conclusion—leave no questions unanswered! That they all live happily ever after is not mandatory, but it sure is nice for the good guy to save the day!

- **Blocking/Timing:** Blocking refers to any stage movement. Did they make use of the stage properly? Were actors running into each other? Was the bulk of the performance directed toward the audience with their viewing pleasure in mind? Were key players turning their backs to the audience while presenting dialogue for no apparent reason? Timing is basically the way the show flows! Was there any dead time? There should be absolutely no one on set for uncomfortably long times, confusion among performers, or any other problems that upset the flow of the show! Misfires could create a blocking/timing problem! Did the performer seem lost or overreact to the misfire? Did the performer cover the problem or make it seem like it was part of the story? If it obviously changed the show for the worse, misfires should be recorded; otherwise if the incident was recovered well, why deduct for it?

- **Acting:** This includes all verbal and nonverbal expression! Were the characters believable? Did they fumble or flub lines? Were they saying the words or did they seem more like they were reading dialogue from the script? Could you feel their pain, sorrow, anger, and happiness?

Judges' Introduction—Before every skit, members of the troop introduce themselves and the characters they play for the panel of judges. This allows the judges to specifically note what the actors are doing wrong or well.

- **Vocal Projection:** Each performer with dialogue must be heard! If it is important for the script, it is important for the story! Did the actors talk to each other or to the audience? Could the audience hear the performance?

Historical Accuracy

Judges are instructed to look for these items for historical accuracy. These elements should also be major considerations in any historical reenactment:

- **Events/Timeline:** Are the facts used in the performance (i.e., dates, places, names) correct?
- **Characters:** Are characters true to the storyline and believable?
- **Dialogue:** Avoid modern dialogue, slang, and references. You can still tell a good political joke—just use President Grant instead of President Bush! Autos are buggies, buses are stagecoaches, and trains by coincidence are still trains!
- **Props:** Buckets, brooms, chairs, bottles, tools, saddles, locks, keys, or anything else on the set is eligible for scrutiny! All trappings and accoutrements must be period-correct, constructed to duplicate actual items in existence, or must be a suitable RGA-approved reproduction. For example, vests without full collars are approved, and elastic suspenders are approved but must be worn under a vest.
- **Garments:** Shirts, britches, vests, dresses, blouses, coats, and jackets. No modern tags should be showing!
- **Head/footwear:** Boots, brogans, loggers shoes, moccasins, sandals, and ladies shoes.
- **Accessories:** Spurs, chaps, watches, badges, parasols, jewelry, makeup, fans, purses, and glasses.
- **Weapons and Rigs:** Weapons and support equipment should be representative of the time period. For Old West reenactment, this means that Ruger Vaqueros are suitable reproductions, but Ruger Super Blackhawks are not! Also, the bird's head grips do have obvious restrictions. The Cimarron Arms Lightning or Thunder do resemble the original Colt Lightning, and even though they are not double action, they are deemed acceptable. The various Uberti and Ruger bird's head grip styles are not. Research the difference in styles. Rugers are not suitable for strict historical reenactments even though they are allowed by this organization in its events.

Production Guidance

Know and follow all rules of firearms safety. These rules are strict and point deductions for violations are often given by the judges.

Keep your reenactment group small, with no more than ten troop members until you have performance experience. The more reenactors you have, the more likely an error and point reduction.

Although props can greatly enhance a presentation, be very careful about using props that are sensitive to weather, difficult to move, overly complicated, or potential distractions from the presentation. Keep your props simple and mobile.

Center your performances on your best actors and use new people for bit parts. Allow the new people to work their way up the chain.

Write your presentation so that supporting characters can be dropped from the sketch to accept the roles of lead characters that may be absent. Have a backup skit prepared in case cast members are not present.

Do not crowd your time limit. Practice you skit under the clock several times before the performance.

Sheriff Foils the Robbery—A Wild and Wooly West troop member plays a sheriff gathering up the gold after a robbery attempt.

At the end of a presentation it is normal for the judges to question the cast members. Interview each other and look for historical problems. Decide on your answers to the judges' questions before the performance. If you believe you will be challenged, bring historical evidence to the performance to support your claims. Sometimes judges are not sure and want your input. Failure to have any answer will cost you points.

Be mindful of offensive language, characters, and implications. Racial, ethnic, sexist, and religious comments can be offensive to modern audiences even if historically accurate. Be mindful of your audience and children regarding all dialogue and storylines.

Old West Reenactment

If you enjoy the history of the Old West, attending these events can be quite entertaining. Preparing and presenting characters and dramatic presentations of the Old West is an excellent way to share our national heritage while allowing the amateur and professional historian alike to learn and exchange knowledge.

Index

XYZ